84

A Life with Old Labs

Lab Love ♡
Barbara Osgood

84 Paws

A Life with Old Labs

Barbara Travis Osgood

Keep up with **84 Paws** at: www.84paws.com

ISBN: 9781095298909

This book is dedicated to those whose lives are devoted to rescuing animals in need.

A portion of the proceeds from the sale of this book will go to Lab Rescue LRCP for the rescue and care of senior labs.

FOREWORD

Several years ago, on a bright Saturday morning, I attended my first adoption event as a volunteer for Lab Rescue LRCP. It was noisy and chaotic, with several dozen volunteers and potential adopters milling around a PetSmart parking lot. There were labs of all shapes and sizes; and, the hair, drool, and water bowls were flying everywhere. Into this fray pulled a car with a vanity plate that read simply, OLD LABS. A rather striking woman got out of the car. She calmly and lovingly assisted her elderly charge out of the car, and got him quietly set up in a nice shady spot. In the midst of a lot of crazy, Barbara Osgood was unfazed.

Over the next few years, it was my privilege to spend more than our fair share of Saturday mornings together. Barbara was known as "The Old Lab Lady." She was our go-to person when an older lab entered the rescue. She was a foster, an adopter, and an outspoken advocate for the rehoming of senior labs. She could extol the virtues of adopting an older lab to anyone who would listen. As I got to know her, I learned she was keenly intelligent, had a wicked sense of humor, and did not suffer fools gladly. I could rely on her for frank advice and a soft shoulder. Rescue work is hard: it certainly takes a toll on those involved, and Barbara always made it somehow easier.

A few years into our friendship, while shooting a short documentary about "The Old Lab Lady," Barbara very matter-of-factly mentioned she was bipolar. I was, to put it mildly, taken aback as I had had no inkling that she fought mental illness. She was always so strong, so compassionate, so kind. I had never realized she was fighting an inner battle that most of us can ever understand. I had a history with bipolar disorder: I had watched helplessly as it consumed someone who was close to me. That person did not survive the constant depression, the self-questioning, the outright hopelessness from which many never escape. To learn that Barbara suffered for years from all those things was, to me, heartbreaking. To know that she somehow found a way to survive was—and is—uplifting.

84 Paws is more than a story about saving elderly labs. It is the story about a woman, who, against all odds, saved herself. It chronicles her life, her loss of family, her struggle to complete an education, her fight to achieve a respected place in a male-dominated work culture, her enormous successes as well as her heart-wrenching plunges into darkness. It is frank, humorous, and illuminating. It outlines the painful journey to survive and overcome. It introduces the reader to a cast of funny, furry, feisty, senior labs who have occupied Barbara's home and heart.

I was lucky to know a few of Barbara's old labs, and they were as charming—and as stubborn—as she portrays them. Barbara was told by a medical professional that she would never find the love she sought, but her labs certainly proved that person wrong. By having the courage to simply keep going, to fight for herself, to defy old conventions of gender and background, Barbara survived. She turned her love of labs into the best of all possible therapies. Love heals. A lesson she learned from observing one of her more severely traumatized old labs: "I learned that no matter how bad things might seem, if you can find something soft and fuzzy to hug, your heart will start to mend." As her book demonstrates, Barbara found many soft and fuzzy things to hug. Her resilience is proof that her heart has gone a long way toward mending.

Kathy Feininger

Chief Creative Officer, Chanticleer Productions LLP

Former Director of Education and Outreach, Round House Theater

Westport, MA

TABLE OF CONTENTS

BEGINNINGS

Dogs are our link to paradise... To sit with a dog on a hillside on a glorious afternoon is to be back in Eden, where doing nothing was not boring—it was peace.

Milan Kundera

Dogs have been sharing their lives with us for thousands of years. We will never know exactly what caused that first wolf/dog to throw his fate in with early humans, but, whatever the reason, it was an auspicious one—not only for the dog, but also for us.

Science has documented the physical ways that dogs are good for the people who live with them. When we pet a dog, our blood pressure is lowered. When we look into her eyes, our levels of oxytocin soar, and we feel good. When we are greeted by a joyous dog after a long day of work, our spirits are lifted.

We see the roles that dogs play in the well-being of humans every day. The dog that guides his blind mistress across a city street. The dog that finds a lost child. The dog that signals when a seizure is imminent. Dogs that provide comfort and support to veterans with PTSD. Dogs that perform tasks for the deaf and the wheelchair bound.

It remains for someone to invent the analytical technique that can measure the many intangible benefits of life with dogs—benefits that derive from their range of emotions, their ability to "read" our state of mind, their desire to please, and, for want of a better term, their "philosophy of life." Those of us who love dogs just know that it is better to live with them than without them.

This book is the story of my life with old rescued Labrador Retrievers: strays that were picked up by Animal Control, shelter dogs given up by their owners for one reason or another, breeder dogs that had outlived their usefulness, abandoned dogs. They are the dogs that, all too often, are euthanized because no one wants them. They have found a home with me for over more than twenty years. Twenty-one labs. Eighty-four paws. All have enriched my life in their own special ways.

My dogs have not only been loyal companions: they have also given me the love and support I have needed to survive bipolar illness. They have been my therapists as well as my family.

STARS IN THE VOID

It is not an easy thing—maybe the work of a lifetime—to live as if we are loved. To quiet the voices of self-condemnation. To live outside the tiny cosmos of our own desires. To extend the grace we have been shown.

Michael Gerson

The story of my dogs might have started in a breeder's kennel with a litter of newborn puppies. Or it might have started in a county animal shelter, where an old dog, abandoned by his owners, waited to be adopted. But my dog story didn't begin in a kennel or a shelter. It began in a psychiatrist's office.

Ever since my first major depression, psychiatrists have been a part of my life. They have come and gone, like actors in a play—some only in bit parts, a few in supporting roles.

There was the doctor who recommended that I "go out for dinner and think happy thoughts."

The one who prescribed medication that gave me amnesia.

The one who handed me a baseball bat and told me to "beat up that pillow like you mean it."

They were the bit players.

Enter Dr. Khoury, who took my case when I was hospitalized after a suicide attempt. He questioned me for hours every day, leaning back in his leather chair and jotting notes on the clipboard balanced on his knee. Reluctantly, I shared bits and pieces of my life with him—things that I had never told anyone before:

"I feel like I'm living on a roller coaster."

"I can't sleep, so I get in my car and drive all night."

"There have been men—some of them I didn't even know."

"I sink into deep depressions when all I want to do is kill myself to ease the pain."

For a week, Dr. Khoury listened to my story without comment, bent over his notes, occasionally asking me to clarify a thought. Then he gave me his diagnosis:

"I'm sure you have bipolar disorder. It's a mental illness that brings severe high and low moods. You have displayed all of the classic symptoms."

He looked up at me to check my reaction.

I was elated.

All those years of suffering and not knowing what was wrong with me. A failed marriage. An alienated family. Lost friendships. For the first time my malady had a name. It was real. I needed to know more.

"What comes next?"

Dr. Khoury put down his clipboard and shifted in his chair to lean toward me.

"It's a difficult disease, but there are medication and therapy. You can hope to lead a relatively normal life."

His diagnosis was a gift, even though I knew it was only the beginning of a long and uncertain journey.

* * *

Years later, another major actor came onto the scene. Her name was Dr. Elkes. She led me back once again from the brink of suicide. I was still searching for the stability of a relatively normal life.

Dr. Elkes explained how my need to be loved shaped relationships that often led to physical and emotional abuse, followed by depression.

"You are the stereotypical abused woman. You will do anything, and tolerate any treatment, just to feel that you are loved."

Her diagnosis was no less bleak than Dr. Khoury's.

"Barbara, you will never be loved the way you want to be loved. Because of your childhood experiences, you have a void inside you that will never be filled. You will just have to live with it. You will find a way."

I moved away and never saw Dr. Elkes again, but her blunt words stayed with me through more years of heartache and failed relationships—my futile search to fill the void.

Then one day, the search ended in a way that neither I nor Dr. Elkes would have predicted.

How amazing to discover that the void would not be filled by another human being, but by loving creatures with four legs, fur, and wet noses.

They are the stars of my drama.

THE END OF THE BEGINNING

Do you not see how necessary a world of pains and troubles is to school an intelligence and make it a soul?

John Keats

May 26, 1980. Cornell University commencement. The doctoral candidates in red robes took their places at the front of the line. The procession began.

But I wasn't there. I was lying on a bed in a stark white hospital room in the mental health wing of Georgetown Hospital. My bed and a small table were the only furnishings in the room. My clothes and possessions had been stripped away. Through the window in my locked door, I could see someone sitting on a chair just outside. I was on suicide watch.

I had dreamed of commencement for years. It would be a beautiful spring day in Ithaca, the sun glinting from the white-tipped waves of Lake Cayuga. The campus would be alive with thousands of graduates and their families, chattering and laughing, savoring the joy of the special day. I pictured myself joining the other doctoral candidates at the front of the academic procession. We would lead the way like a flock of scarlet birds in our red robes trimmed with black velvet.

My beautiful dream had evaporated. There would be no joyous commencement celebration, no memorable photos with my proud family. Instead I would spend the next seven weeks in the hospital with more than enough time to wonder: What would it have been like to wear the red robe trimmed with black velvet? To march in the procession? To feel the weight of the doctoral hood falling onto my shoulders?

* * *

My diploma arrived in the mail a few weeks later. I ran my fingers over the inscription— "Doctor of Philosophy"—thinking about the path I had taken to reach my goal.

A path that covered four years and thousands of miles. A path on which I had lived a double life, commuting every week between my home near New York City and Cornell University in Ithaca. At home, I assumed the role of the stereotypical suburban housewife: managing the household, enjoying family activities, and walking my dog. At Cornell, I became the serious doctoral student: attending classes, and spending late nights in the library, exploring new and fascinating subjects.

The long drive through the Catskill Mountains between New York and Ithaca was my time to leave one role behind and take on the other. Superman had his telephone booth; I had a dark green Chevy Nova.

At first no one seemed to notice—least of all me—that the stress of the routine had begun to change me. My pleasure at being accepted into the doctoral program grew into excitement and then exhilaration. I couldn't sleep—often driving all night to calm the turmoil in my mind. I had energy to spare. I took swimming lessons and skiing lessons. I flew with a friend while he practiced touch and go landings in his Cessna—and even tried piloting the plane. Thoughts ricocheted around my brain like the silver balls in a pinball machine. I seemed to have relentless drive and more courage than I had ever known.

I was fearless. I could accomplish anything. Like someone who has been lost in the desert, and, on being rescued, can't get enough to drink, I was insatiable.

Semester after semester, as I mastered statistics and research methods, wrote term papers and prepared a dissertation, the course of my life spun out of control. The change in my personality eroded my marriage and alienated my family and friends. It never occurred to anyone that I might be mentally ill. Family and friends only knew that I had morphed into an unrecognizable version of my former self. They had no explanation except to say, "Well, she is working very hard."

My best friend warned, "You're acting like someone who's been told she only has six months to live." Then she never spoke to me again.

It would be another ten years before the explanation would come: sleeplessness, agitation, wild thoughts and recklessness—classic symptoms of bipolar disorder.

* * *

My husband finally ran out of patience: "Don't come home."

My tortured brain was too chaotic to argue. *It's my home, too.* I could only give in to the demand, with no idea of what the future might bring.

Like the obedient wife I had been trained to be, I didn't go home.

I didn't return to my bewildered teenage children. I didn't return to the Dutch colonial house that I had lovingly decorated, with its perennial borders and rock gardens that I had planted and cultivated. I didn't return to my beloved yellow Labrador Retriever. I left behind my garden club, my church groups, and my long-time friends. The life that I had lived for more than twenty years was over. The sheltered suburban housewife no longer existed. And no one was around to mourn the loss.

I sat on the bed in my hotel room and once again looked at the words on my diploma. It seemed a strange victory that I could now call myself "Doctor."

Cornell had educated me to do great things. But I was forty-five years old, I was alone for the first time in my life, and I was mentally ill.

METAMORPHOSIS

Who knows what women can be when they are finally free to become themselves.

Betty Friedan

"You are going to be homeless and end up living on the street."

My husband's parting words.

I'd seen a homeless woman for the first time when I was working in the South Bronx. She shuffled along the sidewalk in her baggy thrift-shop clothes, pushing a shopping cart that held everything she owned. People walked around her without making eye contact. Was that my future?

I took inventory. I didn't have a job. I had a car, an office full of books and files, a sparsely furnished apartment on which the rent was due in two weeks, $500 in the bank, and a piece of paper that said I was a PhD.

It was more than a shopping cart, but it wasn't much.

Living on the street looked like a real possibility.

* * *

I wasn't raised to be an independent woman. I was brought up to be a "good girl"—a "lady" in my mother's terminology.

"Ladies have good manners and know which fork to use."

"Sit quietly and behave like a lady."

There's a portrait of me in 1941 at the age of seven that says it all. I sit stiffly next to my sister in a starched ruffled pinafore. My hair is curled over my shoulders and held back with a white satin ribbon. My hands are posed gracefully in my lap. I am not smiling.

It might have been my mother in 1916, or my grandmother in 1885. Good girls, ladies, all of us, who knew our role in life.

Good little girls started out with the proper toys. Bride dolls with veils and white satin gowns. Baking sets that made real cakes. Miniature cleaning supplies like mops, brooms, and dust pans.

My mother repeatedly reminded me: "A good girl doesn't climb trees, hang upside down from the monkey bars on the jungle gym, or fill a Mason jar with bugs."

Girls were to be, as the nursery rhyme intoned, *sugar and spice, and everything nice.*

In high school I was a good student. I aced algebra and geometry. But when it was time to move on, my guidance counselor was firm:

"Girls don't take trigonometry."

I got the message. Good girls did not do advanced mathematics.

I didn't take trig.

At Cornell in the early 1950s we were informed that the curriculum would prepare us to be "educated wives and mothers who practiced gracious living."

Someone in authority told us: "You are not to wear pants on campus." So we didn't.

Someone else made the rule: "You must be in the dorm by eleven." So we were.

No one asked why.

I read Chaucer, studied the law of supply and demand, and solved physics problems. But I also learned the best way to wash windows, how to select the correct laundry detergent, and how to iron a man's shirt in seven minutes.

Society had made a bargain with us: be a good girl and a nice man will marry you, put you in a rose-covered cottage, and take care of you forever.

With visions of those rose-covered cottages in our heads, we married early—sometimes even before graduation. We pored over magazines like *Good Housekeeping* and *The Ladies' Home Journal* where our role models were women whose hair and make-up were flawless, whose homes were beautifully decorated, and whose children never misbehaved.

We met for coffee and wondered whether it really did improve a marriage to wrap your naked body in Saran wrap before greeting your husband at the door.

We worried about wrinkles, frosted our hair, and polished our nails. We were living our destiny. We were supposed to be happy.

But while I was busy being the perfect housewife, the world was changing. Betty Friedan challenged us with *The Feminine Mystique.* Gloria Steinem covertly chronicled the life of a Playboy Bunny. Women all over the country burned their bras. Peggy Lee sang "Is That All There Is?"

Like an old earthquake disaster movie where tall buildings crumble into dust before your eyes, the tectonic plates of my life began to shift. What I had always been taught to value—a spotless home, a batch of homemade cookies, a well-turned seam—no longer seemed important.

* * *

I named my yellow Labrador Retriever "Libby" in honor of Women's Lib.

I went back to school for my doctorate. And this time I took trigonometry.

* * *

I had earned my PhD. But outside the sanctuary of the university I found myself in a maelstrom of social change: new life styles, new ideas, new rules—all viewed through the prism of my manic mood. Disturbing questions, fueled by the mania, spun through my mind: *Are good girls gone forever? What does it mean to be a "liberated woman"? Will I survive in this unfamiliar world? Who will take care of me? Who will keep me from being lonely? Who will love me?*

I wasn't raised to be independent, so I would have to learn.

I could become that homeless woman in the South Bronx, or learn to take care of myself.

I could mourn the loss of the rose-covered cottage, or create my own future.

I could return to the safety of the cocoon where I was raised. Or I could burst free of its constraints, and spread the wings I was meant to use.

I decided to fly.

BLAZING TRAILS

An intelligent, energetic, educated woman cannot be kept in four walls—even satin-lined, diamond-studded walls—without discovering sooner or later that they are still a prison cell.

Pearl S. Buck

"You're the first, Doctor Osgood. Congratulations. You're a trailblazer."

I had just been hired by the Chief of the Soil Conservation Service.

"We've had a lot of engineers, economists, and soil scientists over the years but we've never had a sociologist. We need someone to help our professionals understand the farmers and ranchers they work with."

"And you'll also be one of the first women. Until now, we've been an all-male agency, but change is coming to the Department of Agriculture."

He shrugged and chuckled. I wasn't sure what that meant.

It didn't matter. I couldn't wait to get started.

Blazing a trail seemed like a great idea.

* * *

Like Heinlein's hero, I was a stranger in a strange land. I shared gender with the secretaries, but they understood that I had a different role. I needed to join the boys' team. But how?

They were a fraternity of men who had grown up on farms and ranches. They went fishing and hunting together. They shared the same experiences. They spoke the same language. It would not be easy to join their ranks.

I could see right away that office routine was important, especially when it came to lunch. No matter what the men were doing, lunch began at 11:30 and ended promptly at noon.

In a meeting? "It's 11:30. We need to break for lunch."

At your desk? When the hands on the clock got to eleven and six, it was time to drop what you were doing and join the parade to the cafeteria.

For everyone but me. My first days on the job, the Great Lunch Exodus took place without so much as a *Would you like to join us, Barbara?* Thinking I was too new to invite myself, I stood by while the men left the meeting or walked out of my office in the middle of a conversation. I was invisible.

Do they think I don't eat?

I needed to do something. Maybe humor would help?

I sent a memo to the staff:

> *To Whom It May Concern:*
>
> *I am available for lunch. I do not have any dietary constraints. I have good table manners and I chew with my mouth closed. I am also a reasonably good conversationalist and I know the difference between a touchdown and a first down. I would enjoy your company.*
>
> *Barbara*

Days passed, and the lunch routine went on as usual. Just as I was thinking, *Uh-Oh! I have really screwed up*, my office door opened.

"Hey, Barb. Would you like to grab some lunch?"

Lunch looked a little different after that, but it still happened, every day, promptly at 11:30.

And no one ever mentioned the memo.

* * *

I had a lot to learn, and my colleagues were happy to help.

"It's soil, not dirt, Barbara."

"Loess isn't a person. It's a kind of soil."

But no one told me that a sense of humor would be my key to success.

* * *

The motel had seen better days but appeared neat and freshly painted. The men didn't really care where they stayed at night as long as there was enough per diem left over for beer and a steak dinner. My standards were a little higher, and after a couple of experiences with cobwebs and bugs I made it known that I wasn't staying in any more questionable motels.

I made declarations like this cautiously, not wanting to look like I was playing the woman card. But no one had objected. They didn't like cobwebs and bugs in their motel rooms either.

Our team—seven men and I—piled out of our van onto the pavement of the motel parking lot, happy to be out in the open after a long drive. We filed into the motel office.

The middle-aged woman at the counter looked us over and gave me a curious stare.

"Are you all checking in?"

There was a "Yes" from one of the men, and she shuffled paperwork from under the counter.

"All single rooms?" Another "Yes" from our leader.

As she handed out our keys, the clerk's curiosity finally got the better of her. She looked at me with a scowl.

"What are you doing here with all these men?"

"I'm the Den Mother. I watch them for their wives while they are on the road, so that they don't get into any trouble."

Someone in the group snickered.

The clerk nodded with an understanding look, smiling in silent agreement that these men probably could use some looking after.

That evening, as we enjoyed our steaks and beer, the men got their revenge.

"Well, Mom, are you going to tell us how much beer we can drink?"

"Mom, do I have to eat my vegetables?"

Back in the office after our trip, I saw something shiny on my desk. A gold paper crown, labeled MOM in large black letters. I laughed and put it on.

I had blazed a trail. It wasn't the boys' team any more.

* * *

Every Monday morning, suitcase in one hand and briefcase in the other, I took off from the airport for a new destination … a potato farm in Maine … a ranch in California … a dairy in Wisconsin … a town with a flooding problem in southern Arizona … a seminar in Texas.

I loved traveling to parts of the country that tourists never see. And I loved working with the people who lived there. But after a few years it was time for a change. There were other trails to blaze.

I wanted a home.

I wanted a social life.

I wanted a dog.

FINDING PARADISE

Dogs have a way of finding the people who need them, filling an emptiness we don't even know we have.

Thom Jones

I named him Moody.

Not because he was, but because he would keep me from being.

I saw him sitting like a black Sphinx on the floor of the pet store, waiting for someone to adopt him. I crouched in front of him and held out my hand. "Hi there big boy." He studied me with warm brown eyes, but ignored my hand.

I'm not one of those dogs that panders to humans. I won't lick your hand or slobber on you or jump in your lap. I'm a dignified dog. If you want that kind of dog, I'm yours.

The adoption coordinator hovered. "What do you think, Barbara?"

"He's so handsome. He reminds me of an elegant older gentleman who is a little down on his luck right now."

He allowed me to scratch his ears.

Well, are you going to be the lucky human who takes me home or not?

I clipped my leash on his collar. "Let's go home, Moody."

* * *

The rescue told me to crate my dog while I was at work. So Monday morning I ushered Moody into the crate and closed the latch. He curled up without protest. But that evening, he greeted me at the door.

Did you think a clever fellow like me wouldn't know how to open the latch?

The next morning, I was determined to make sure he stayed in the crate, so I twisted a piece of wire around the door.

"You're supposed to stay in the crate, Mister."

He gave me an innocent look, no doubt already planning his escape. Sure enough, that evening he met me at the door again—eyes gleaming, tail wagging. He was enjoying the game.

This is fun. Shall we try it again tomorrow?

Tomorrow never came for the crate. We retired it to storage.

I don't know what Moody did in the hours that I was at work. He never made a mess. He never chewed anything or tried to get into food. He seemed content to hang out until I got home. But he had his limits. When I stayed away too long, he sent a "Moody Message."

> I'm too dignified to chew things up, like other dogs. I just take one of my human's stuffed toys off her bed and put it in the middle of the living room floor. No damage. Only the slightest trace of dog saliva.

If I opened the front door to be greeted by Eeyore's beady eyes, or Raggedy Ann's vacant stare, I knew I was in trouble with the man/dog of the house. Moody was already shaping my life.

* * *

Not long after I brought Moody home, a familiar feeling returned. I tried to shake it off, but it wouldn't let me go. The Lead Blanket. I knew it well.

My body felt as if it weighed hundreds of pounds. Getting out of bed was a struggle. It was easier to stay there, pull the covers over my head, and try to shut out everything around me.

Except that I couldn't shut down my brain. Black thoughts took over my mind like a flock of crows cackling their painful messages: *You are worthless. No one cares about you. No one loves you.* And while a tiny part of my brain tried to maintain that none of it was true, it didn't have a chance against the force of the attack.

Even Moody's cold nose and gentle nudges couldn't change my mood.

I needed to go somewhere—anywhere—to escape.

"There's a street fair in Charlottesville, sweet boy. Let's go stay at the Omni Hotel. They welcome dogs."

> I can tell you aren't happy. Maybe this trip will make you happy.

* * *

The young man who checked us in at the front desk was friendly and attentive, and he liked my companion.

"What a great-looking dog! What's his name?"

"His name is Moody. I just recently adopted him. And yes, he is a sweetheart."

"Well, welcome to the Omni Hotel, big boy." He bent down and gave Moody a dog biscuit.

> This looks like a pretty nice place. I'm glad to be here—especially if the beds are comfortable.

Moody and I set out to enjoy the street fair. It was a warm and humid evening. A few stars were beginning to appear as we strolled down the wide path from the hotel into the noisy colorful atmosphere. Food booths taunted with aromas of ethnic foods. Crafters displayed handmade jewelry and art. Musicians strummed their guitars. I bought an ice cream cone for me and one for Moody.

The fair was crowded. We were surrounded by families surveying the food tents to make their selections, couples strolling hand-in-hand, groups of young women laughing and whispering to each other, teenagers hoping to be noticed.

It should have been an idyllic evening.

There was no escape from the depression. It changed the colors to gray, turned the music into a clash of sour notes, and twisted the tender moments into self-hatred. *Why don't I have happiness in my life like the people around me? Why doesn't anyone care about me?*

In the midst of the crowd, loneliness consumed my thoughts and magnified my depression.

I took Moody back to the hotel room. By now my anxiety had become a driving force. I needed relief. Moody lay on the floor while I frantically searched the room for something sharp. No knives. No razor blades. I dug a heavy duty nail clipper out of my travel kit and used it to make ragged cuts in my wrists.

Moody pawed at me and whined. He licked my wounds. He began to bark.

Something is very wrong here.

His concern broke through the wall of my depression.

"Oh, my God, my sweet boy. I'm so ashamed. I wasn't thinking of you. I was only thinking of myself. I've failed you."

"I won't do this to you again, Moody—ever. I promise. No matter how bad I feel."

Someone heard Moody's frantic barking.

The EMTs took me to the hospital.

The young man from the front desk took care of Moody.

* * *

Back home, Moody knew that I needed him. He slept close to me at night, his rhythmic snoring next to my head like a peaceful lullaby. During the day, when I sat reading and writing in my journal, he curled up next to my chair. It felt good to stroke his silky ears, run my hand over his thick black coat, and feel his rough tongue on my fingers.

"Sweet boy, I don't know what your life was like before we met, but you certainly know how to take care of your human."

We walked for miles. Moody liked to carry a toy in his mouth. His favorite was a large stuffed dog bone. He soon became a center of attention. People smiled when they passed us on the street. Sometimes they stopped to ask about him. Who was this big black dog, trotting along the sidewalk, head held high, carrying his own toy?

Moody became my ambassador to the land of the living.

After a while, I was able to smile back.

And then we added another family member.

ENTER DOCTOR FREUD

Isn't it wonderful how dogs can win friends and influence people without ever reading a book.

Charles E. McKenzie

Barbara wait—don't leave!"

The Lab Rescue volunteer ran toward me across the parking lot, pulling a large white Lab that struggled to keep up with her. He panted and coughed, his pink tongue dangling.

"We have a dog that doesn't have a foster home. Can you take him?"

He was a caricature of a Lab with an expression on his face that warned of imminent mischief. His bowed legs made him walk like a Chinese woman whose feet had been bound. He would not win any prizes at the dog show.

"Sure, I'll take him. Moody would be happy to have a visitor."

It was love at first sight. I knew that he wouldn't be a visitor for long. On the drive home I was already thinking about a name for him.

"Siggy." Short for Sigmund Freud. The perfect complement to Moody.

> Siggy? Like a cigar? Ate one of them once. Tasted like burnt skunk.

He curled up on the dog bed in the back seat and went to sleep.

* * *

Siggy and Moody became instant friends. Siggy brought out Moody's inner puppy, and the two were soon rolling around the floor in mock battle and playing tug of war with the rope toy. My quiet, dignified, black boy was transformed.

Siggy joined us in bed that night, his snores blending with Moody's in a mellow evensong.

> Moody takes up a lotta room. She's gonna need a bigger bed.

He stretched out to claim more of the bed for himself.

* * *

Food was Priority One for Siggy. No one knew how long he had fended for himself as a stray on the streets of Baltimore, but in that time he had developed excellent survival skills. Nothing remotely edible was safe from his grasp.

When the dog sitter opened the refrigerator, he grabbed a baked potato from the shelf, swallowing it whole in seconds.

> Potatoes are okay but I'm watchin' for better stuff next time the door opens.

Clearing the table after dinner became a stealth operation. Siggy could catch a pork chop bone on its way from the dinner plate to the garbage can like a magician making a rabbit disappear.

> Company for dinner? Jackpot!

Siggy was never far from the table at dinner, waiting hopefully for any item of food that might make its way to the floor. No need to clean the floor when Siggy was on duty.

Outdoors was no better. Siggy was like a doggy vacuum cleaner, sucking up anything in his path that appealed to him. A dried squirrel carcass in the street. Canada goose poop (we had to change our route when the geese were around). Discarded remains of fast food meals along with the wrappers. Grass. Bird seed.

> Love to go for walks. It's a banquet out there!

One day Siggy plunged into the bushes just as we walked out the door. He surfaced to sit in front of me with a quizzical expression—and a bird wing sticking out of each side of his mouth. I opened his jaws and freed a baby bird, unhurt, from his soft grasp.

"Siggy, we don't eat things that are still alive."

Oh, well. It seemed like a good idea at the time.

Siggy loved ice cubes. No matter where he was in the house, he could hear the rattle of the ice maker and came running. He crunched his frozen bounty with a faraway look in his eyes, like a connoisseur savoring a fine wine.

His unorthodox eating habits meant that Siggy and I were frequent visitors at the local veterinary emergency clinic. Each time, the staff and I shared a laugh at his latest adventure. Even when he had been a bad boy, we couldn't resist his soulful looks. Was he apologizing?

Gosh, folks. I was just doin' what comes naturally.

Siggy was an expert at looking contrite.

* * *

Even now, more than twenty years later, I think of Siggy every time I pass a certain open space on Route 95 north of Baltimore.

We were on our way to visit family in New York—Moody, Siggy, and I—when Siggy signaled that he had to pee.

"Sorry, Buddy. We're in the Fort McHenry Tunnel. No place to go around here. I'll stop as soon as I can. You'll just have to wait."

Just so ya know, my legs are crossed back here.

Miles went by and Siggy's pleas became more urgent, but I couldn't find a place to pull off the highway. Finally there was an open space, and I eased the SUV off the pavement onto the grass.

"I'm not sure it's legal to stop here, Siggy, but this is the best I can do."

I was walking back to open the hatch when a Maryland State Police car pulled in behind me, blue lights flashing.

"Officer, I'm not sure I was supposed to pull over here, but my dog needs to pee, and this is the first chance I've had to get off the highway."

He looked into the open hatch. "It's OK. Which one has to go?"

"Siggy—the white one. He's an older gentleman and can't always hold it. But I have to be careful, because I don't want Moody—the black one—to get out."

"Well, I'll just stand here and hold on to Moody while Siggy does his business."

He stood next to the hatch with one hand on Moody. The lights reflected the details of his uniform. It looked as if Moody had an armed guard.

Siggy and I took a short walk, and I got ready to load him back into the SUV.

The officer turned toward us. "He's a big boy. Let me put him in the car for you."

"You'll be covered with dog hair."

He chuckled. "It's all part of the job. I'll keep the lights flashing until you get back on the highway."

I drove off hoping that somewhere in his police car he could find a sticky roller.

Now, when I see a Maryland State Police car, I think of that officer who definitely went above and beyond the call of duty.

* * *

My favorite memory of Siggy came later in his life, when old age and arthritis had slowed him down.

The dogs and I were staying in a hotel that had an elegant lobby, with what seemed like acres of polished floor. Siggy struggled to make his way from the front door to the desk, but he might as well have been on an ice rink. His legs splayed in all directions as I tried to hold him up. The bell man, waiting at his stand for the next customer, saw our problem.

"Hey, I think I can help you, big boy."

He came toward us, pulling a large brass luggage cart.

"Here, Siggy. Would you like to ride on this?"

Siggy climbed onto the cart. He looked around the lobby, and rested his head on the crossbar.

Now this is the way to travel.

For the rest of our stay at the hotel, Siggy rode the luggage cart. He looked like an emperor surveying his domain. The hotel guests laughed and clapped and stopped to pet him. He loved being the center of attention.

That memory will stay in my heart forever. My sweet Siggy. The comic. The gourmand. The ruler of all he surveyed.

Riding his golden chariot.

The street urchin had been transformed.

ODE TO JOY

Joyful, joyful, joyful, as only dogs know how to be happy

Pablo Neruda

There are people who say dogs don't have emotions.

They are wrong.

A dog named Buddy told me.

* * *

Living with Moody and Siggy taught me to love the big old boys. They enjoyed their leisurely walks to the local bagel shop. They never missed an opportunity to lounge on the soft sofa cushions. They were like a couple of elderly men spending their golden years in a full-service retirement home.

Chase a squirrel?

> Why bother? They only get away.

Bark at the mailman?

> I'm taking a nap.

Dinner?

> We'll be right there!

The three of us were a family. Two homeless old guys had found their forever home. I traded a lonely and quiet house for one that was busy, sometimes noisy, and always in need of vacuuming. These gray-bearded guys, who savored their ear scratches and tummy rubs, gave me a reason to get up in the morning—even if it was only to run the vacuum.

But just when I thought our family was complete, another big old boy came along—a handsome, fox-red stray named Buddy.

Buddy was supposed to be a foster dog, but he settled into the household as if he had always been there. Despite his age, he loved to play. He teased Moody and Siggy until they got up off their beds and joined his games. He chased tennis balls until I couldn't throw any more. He tried out every toy in the dog basket—chewing, shaking, and tugging. I nicknamed him "Playboy."

> Moody and Siggy are a couple of old fogeys, but if I jump on them, I can get their attention.

* * *

The rescue expected me to bring Buddy to an adoption day so that he could meet prospective adopters. I didn't want to take him. I tried to think of excuses not to go.

But when the day came, we stood with the other foster dogs in the parking lot of the pet store, waiting for adopters to arrive. A middle-aged couple petted Buddy's thick rust-colored coat.

"He's a handsome dog. How old is he?"

"I think he is about 9 years old. He'd be considered a senior."

"We've never adopted a senior dog."

"Well, he has some arthritis, and that will only get worse with age. Then he probably won't be able to go up and down stairs or take long walks. Do you have stairs in your house?"

The couple thanked me and rushed off to look at other dogs.

Why did she say that? I hardly have any arthritis at all.

To my relief no one else was interested in Buddy. I loaded him in the car, drove home, and let the rescue know that he was taken.

Moody and Siggy greeted him like a long lost friend.

My family was complete. Three big old boys. Special boys. My "Three Labketeers."

* * *

Due to some apparent failure in their upbringing, my children have never shared my passion for Labs. Oh, they like them all right, but they don't love them. And they never miss an opportunity to give me a hard time about what they consider to be my canine obsession.

It is Thanksgiving Day. The family has arrived for dinner. I am ready. I have shampooed the carpets. I have saturated the house with air freshener. Scented candles are burning in strategic locations.

"This house smells like dogs."

I can't win.

Looking for love in all the wrong places, Moody, Siggy, and Buddy greet the family with wagging tails and uplifted muzzles.

> We are so handsome and lovable. You are welcome to pet us at any time.

The family responds with absent-minded pats on the head. They are focused more on dinner preparations than on canine social interactions. They don't notice that in passing they have been anointed with strands of dog hair and dollops of drool. Moody, Siggy, and Buddy know how to make their presence known.

* * *

Dinner is served.

The dogs have taken their places under the table, hoping that some tasty morsel will make its way to the floor. Or maybe someone, in a weak moment, will pass a piece of turkey within their reach.

We pull out our chairs to sit down.

"Where's Buddy?" My son is the first to notice. "Siggy and Moody are under the table, but Buddy isn't here."

Now everyone was looking. "Where can he be?" "I don't see him anywhere."

"He should be under the table with the other dogs." I knew the three were always together.

Then I remembered.

An hour earlier, I had let the dogs out into the backyard. When they came back inside, Buddy must have been left behind.

I ran downstairs to the back door. Buddy stood in the frigid November air, looking through the glass. When he saw me his tail wagged—slowly at first, and then at top speed.

She came! She came! I thought she was never coming back.

I opened the door. "Oh, Buddy, I ...."

Buddy didn't wait for me to finish my sentence. He was inside in a flash.

He ran. He sprinted up the stairs to the main floor, taking them two at a time.

He bolted like a dog on fire from one end of the house to the other, skidding to a stop at the wall, whirling around, legs flailing, reversing direction.

Back and forth. Back and forth. Long pink tongue flapping from the side of his mouth. Eyes sparkling.

Until he collapsed in a panting drooling heap at my feet.

Oh, happy day! She didn't forget me!

Joy. Pure joy. Buddy's joy.

And mine.

KIBBLE AND BISCUITS

You can trust your dog to guard your house, but never trust your dog to guard your sandwich.

Anonymous

Do you eat to live or live to eat?

"Eat only to live," Benjamin Franklin admonished.

But a Labrador Retriever would give a different answer:

Do I have to make a choice?

To a Lab, food is Nirvana. It is Paradise. It is the pot of kibble at the end of the rainbow.

At my house, a downstairs bathroom is the sacred ground for this canine passion. There, like a chef at Le Cordon Bleu, I prepare the *menu du jour* for each dog. I've been doing it for more than twenty years, for twenty-one dogs and an unknown number of foster dogs.

The basic recipe is kibble. But just as a chef prepares variations on a theme, the kibble is just a start. A Lab would happily eat the same plain brown bits twice a day, every day, for the rest of his life. It is the human/chef in me that says, "That must be so boring."

I have a mental image of a Lab looking at his bowl and, like the husband in a TV sitcom, saying:

> What? This again?

So the kibble gets variations: kibble with canned food, kibble with boiled chicken breast, kibble with ground beef, kibble with shredded "dog salami."

There is a different menu for the times when a dog has an upset tummy. The kibble becomes rice. Rice with strained chicken baby food. Rice with boiled hamburger. Rice with cottage cheese. Rice with chicken broth.

And then there are the medications, served in a piece of cheese. Glucosamine to prevent arthritis. Non-steroid anti-inflammatories and pain killers for the discomfort of arthritis. Pills for old ladies with weak bladders. Tranquilizers for the dogs that need them.

The offerings are served on the altar of the bathroom sink. The right bowl for the right dog in the right place. Bizzy had to eat in her crate because she was a food guarder. Molly eats behind a gate, because she gobbles her food and will eat everyone else's too. New dogs always eat alone until their food manners are revealed.

* * *

Molly weighs 110 pounds. She should weigh less. I fill her bowl with half a ration of kibble and add green beans to make up the difference. There's a probiotic supplement to ease her digestion, and a spoonful of canned chicken. I hope the aroma will help her forget the bowl isn't as full as usual.

Daffy has had surgery for laryngeal paralysis. She has a hole in her throat that never closes. I stir canned food into her kibble so that it is coated and sticky and clings together. She eats it slowly. She coughs and wheezes while I pray the food isn't going into her lungs. Sometimes she waits for me to hand-feed her as I did after the surgery. I don't mind. She is thirteen years old, and she is special.

* * *

The sacred space of the bathroom was always Hope's domain. Like a high priestess of food, only she could cross the threshold to stand at my feet while I fixed dinner. The other dogs knew they had to wait outside the door. New arrivals learned Hope's rules, or suffered the consequences.

Bizzy was a new arrival.

I was filling the bowls when I heard a strangled yelp behind me. Like a furry black beetle, Bizzy was on her back, legs flailing.

Hope stood over her, nose to nose, staring into her startled eyes. There had been no growling or barking. No drama. Just a silent and swift pinning of Bizzy to the floor, like the climax of an uneven wrestling match.

She got the message.

But Bizzy soon found a way to mend her damaged ego. She had an undiscovered talent. She could pick up her bowl.

"Bizzy, bring me your bowl."

Whether it was at the back of her crate or in the backyard, Bizzy found her bowl, picked it up, and dropped it at my feet. No other dog could do that. Not even Hope.

Hope's pursuit of food was legendary. She was banished from the kitchen when she learned to empty all the drawers and cupboards. We moved to the family room. It seemed like a good choice. There was no food there. That is, until I installed a small refrigerator for dog food. It had only been in place for a day when Hope opened the door and ate everything.

"We aren't going to have a repeat of the kitchen fiasco, Hope." I spoke to her sternly. She looked contrite.

I wrapped the refrigerator in duct tape. Hope bypassed the duct tape, chewed the rubber gasket from around the door, and helped herself.

The refrigerator was moved to the laundry room. It had a door that Hope couldn't open.

* * *

K.D. was a petite package of black fur and pink tongue. She made up for her lack of size with determination and bluster. She wanted dinner on time. No matter what I was doing, K.D. stood in front of me at four in the afternoon and barked. Not a "What's going on?" bark. A "Do as I say" bark. If the bigger dogs were in her way, she just pushed them aside.

It's time for dinner.

You could set your watch by K.D.

When to eat is important to a Lab.

What to eat is even more important.

Humans think Labs should eat kibble, canned dog food, dog biscuits, cooked chicken, ground beef and other healthy selections.

Labs would add shoes, underwear, socks, TV remotes, anything on the kitchen counter, and whatever can be found on the street. Labs are not called opportunistic feeders for nothing.

I wrote a Facebook story about my foster dog Katie, who loved to drink out of the garden hose. She was an old girl, but she danced like a puppy as the spray from the hose wet her face and she licked the drops from the hose nozzle. I thought it was charming.

"Don't you know dogs shouldn't drink water from a hose? It is bad for them," a Facebook follower wrote.

I didn't tell her that Labs also drink water from lakes and streams, from rainwater downspouts and from murky puddles on the street. Daffy loves to lick the puddles that form on the slate patio. And I have to drag her from the manhole cover behind the house where she finds little reservoirs of rainwater after a storm. Labs are not only opportunistic feeders. They are equal opportunity drinkers.

* * *

Siggy, the former stray, learned to find food in unexpected places. One day he spied a dried squirrel carcass on the street. He grabbed it before I could lure him away. It was firmly clenched in his teeth, but I could see some telltale fragments of squirrel anatomy sticking out from under his lip. He hadn't swallowed it yet. I grabbed his muzzle, forced my fingers between his teeth, and pulled out a squirrel leg.

"Eeew."

Another leg. *"Eeew."*

The tail. *"Double Eeew."*

We must have been a sight for a YouTube video. Siggy, his jaws clenched, clinging to his prize. Me, pulling squirrel pieces out of his mouth, howling in disgust. And, when it was all over, Siggy looking at me with his innocent brown eyes:

> Well, that was kinda fun. But I really did want a taste of that squirrel.

* * *

Taking food from the mouth of a possessive Lab can be a challenge.

I was walking three Labs when Ginger, a new member of the family, found a pork chop bone. I forgot that the other dogs were familiar with my habit of opening their mouths and removing unwanted items. Ginger wasn't. When I pried her jaws apart, she clamped down—not only on the pork chop bone, but also on my finger.

Blood poured from the injured finger. As if on cue, the FedEx truck pulled up next to me. The driver needed my signature.

"*B* will do," he stammered as he reached into the truck for a paper towel to stanch the flow of blood. "*B* will do. You don't have to write your full name."

A few stitches repaired the damage. But I never tried to take a bone from Ginger's mouth again.

* * *

"Leave it" is the official command to keep your dog from picking up something you don't want her to have. The dog has to learn it. And so do I. Sadly, I'm not much more trainable than the dog.

When I see something before the dog senses it, there is time for negotiating. There is time to be relaxed. I remember to say "Leave it." But if the dog sees something before I do, seconds count. I revert to a primal scream, *"Ah, Ah, Ah, Ah, Ah,"* not found in a training manual. The dogs know both sounds mean the same thing, but their response depends on the object in question.

Chewed gum?

> No problem. Didn't really want it anyway.

Melted ice cream?

> I'm probably willing to pass that up.

Chicken bones?

Did somebody say "Leave it?" I can't hear a thing.

Eat to live *and* live to eat. That's a Lab's life.

Mr. Franklin would have been disappointed.

THE RIGHT PLACE

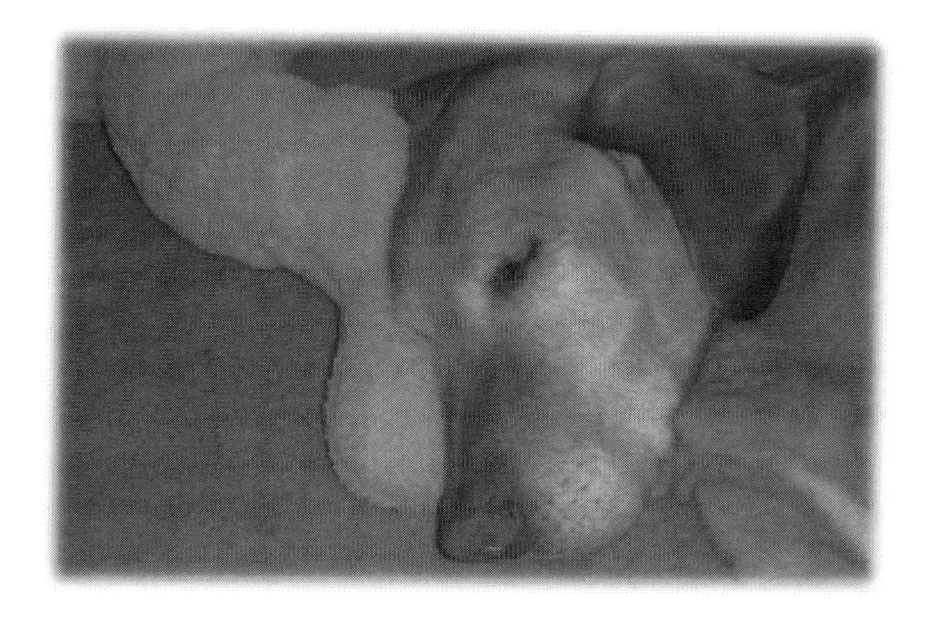

She had no particular breed in mind, no unusual requirements. Except the special sense of mutual recognition that tells dog and human they have both come to the right place.

Lloyd Alexander

The dog came out of the tall weeds lining the side of the road, staggered onto the pavement and collapsed. Her tongue rested on the road surface like a limp scrap of pink cloth. She lay motionless, as if she had used up her last bit of energy to drag herself into the open where she might be seen. She probably sensed that she was near death. But her senses could not have told her that, of all the roads in this western Virginia county, she had found the right one.

Joanna was headed to the grocery store in her van, but her mind wasn't on groceries. She was thinking about the new phone book that had not yet been delivered. All of her neighbors had theirs. She decided her copy must have fallen off the mail truck on its way to her house. She scanned the roadside as she drove along, hoping to see the book with its familiar yellow cover lying in the bushes.

As if in response to her thoughts, something appeared on the road ahead.

She slowed her van, brought it to a stop just short of where it lay, and jumped out. She was so focused on the idea of a phone book that it took her a few seconds to realize what was in front of her—not a phone book but a dog, a yellow Lab lying on the pavement.

Glazed eyes looked up at her from an emaciated body. Shallow breaths came from the dog's throat, but it made no sound, nor did it try to move.

Whether it was Divine Intervention, Karma, or just plain luck, there was no better person than Joanna to arrive at that time, in that place. It never occurred to her to drive away and leave the dog to die. She scooped the limp body up in her arms, loaded her gently in the van, and took off for her veterinarian's office. The phone book was forgotten. She was going to save this dog.

* * *

Two weeks later, in another part of Virginia, I pulled my SUV with its OLD LABS license plates into the parking lot of the pet store where rescuers were setting up for their monthly adoption event. Dogs barked and yelped and pulled at their leashes, already sensing the excitement of the day. I hadn't even turned off the ignition when a couple of volunteers came running toward me, waving their arms:

"We have a Barbara Osgood dog!"

I knew what that meant: an old dog, probably arthritic, and maybe in need of special care. Ever since I started volunteering with Lab Rescue, these were the dogs that fed my soul and gave my life purpose. Dogs that most adopters didn't want. Dogs that often died in the shelter. These were the dogs I took home with me to stay.

I turned the ignition key and got out of the car. "Where's the dog?"

I followed them across the parking lot, weaving through the noisy crowd to a van, parked with its side door open. In the doorway sat a yellow Labrador Retriever, leaning quietly against the slender middle-aged woman who held her leash. The dog's gaunt face and big eyes gave her a waif-like beauty. Her fur was soft and shiny, an amber shade of yellow that, in Lab circles, is called fox red.

The woman called to me. "I'm Joanna. The one who found her. Please come sit with us."

I joined Joanna in the doorway of the van with the Lab between us. I petted her and stroked her ears while Joanna told me the story of the dog she had named Abby Belle.

Joanna's eyes filled with tears.

"I really want to keep her, but I already have too many dogs and cats. I just don't have room for another. I know Lab Rescue will find a good home for her."

By then, my rescue friends had gathered around the van, listening to the story they already knew.

"So, will you take her?"

Will you take her home with you?"

"You know she's your kind of dog!"

How could I say no?

* * *

Starvation had left its mark on Abby. She was hungry all the time. She tried to climb onto the dining room table when we were eating. She pulled pots of boiling food off the stove. Nothing edible was safe unless it was in the refrigerator or behind closed doors. I monitored her eating so she didn't take in too much, too fast. Still, it was good to see her body gradually showing the roundness of a dog that had enough to eat.

Abby quickly found her place in the family and made friends with resident Labs Moody and Siggy. Siggy was her special boy. She slept close to him at night and was never far from him during the day. I often found them snoozing together, back to back, on the big dog bed. Siggy didn't seem to mind her adolescent crush. Maybe he knew she needed a friend.

The house was Abby's to explore. She discovered a spot on the guest room bed where the afternoon sun made a patch of warmth and light on the flowered coverlet. It became her favorite place to curl up and take a nap.

* * *

Soon after Abby arrived, she had a seizure. Without warning her body stiffened. Her eyes glazed. Her tongue, covered with foamy drool, hung limply from her mouth. She urinated and defecated uncontrollably. Spasm after spasm racked her fragile body.

When the spasms ceased, she ran blindly around the house, bumping into furniture and knocking over small tables.

Abby's past was unknown. If the seizures had started when she was a young dog she was probably epileptic. There was medication for that. Seizures starting in her old age could signal a more ominous outcome.

My veterinarian prescribed phenobarbital, and said "Let's see if she has any more."

Abby's seizures continued, growing in frequency and intensity. I had a disaster plan. At the first sign of a seizure, I grabbed some phenobarbital and threw a blanket over her. As soon as it was safe, I pushed the pills down her throat. And before she went blind, I wrapped the blanket tightly around her and lay on top of her. It took all of my strength to keep her from escaping.

One day Abby had a seizure on the front lawn. I was without my usual pills and blanket. We wrestled on the ground while I held desperately to one of her legs, terrified that she would run into the street. The seizure spent, we lay together on the ground, covered with mulch and soil, gasping from the exertion. A neighbor walked by with a quizzical look.

"I have a dog with a seizure here," I called.

"Oh." He kept on walking, oblivious to our trauma. I guess he wasn't a dog person.

The seizures were relentless. An MRI revealed what I didn't want to know. Abby had an inoperable brain tumor. There was no treatment.

Abby lived five more months. She spent Christmas and Easter with my two-year-old granddaughter who hugged her and called her "Abby the Dog." She slept back to back with Siggy in their soft dog bed. She went everywhere with me in the car. She had as much to eat as she wanted.

I treasure the memory of one of Abby's last days. I heard a thumping noise in the guest room, and went to investigate. The sun was shining on the bed, and Abby was trying to jump to her favorite spot. Only she couldn't. She had gained too much weight.

I boosted Abby onto the pink-flowered coverlet. She curled up in her usual spot and rested her head on the ruffled pillow. The sun glistened on her golden-orange fur. She sighed and slipped into a peaceful sleep.

The homeless waif had found her right place.

THE JOURNEY

I think we all suffer from acute blindness at times. Life is a constant journey of trying to open your eyes.

Olivia Thirlby

There's a chocolate Lab in the Minneapolis city shelter. Her name is Maggie Mae. She's blind, and she's terrified. We need to get her out ASAP.

The chat line messages on my computer screen came alive.

Poor baby. Is she diabetic?

The shelter says no. They think she has Progressive Retinal Atrophy.

PRA? Oh, my Lord. Has she been bred?

She's had at least one litter. She's probably a backyard breeder.

And now she's passed the gene on to her puppies. That makes me so angry. A responsible breeder would have tested her before they bred her.

Well, you know how it goes with backyard breeders.

I didn't know much about PRA, so the back and forth of the chat was interesting, but it wasn't getting us any closer to rescuing Maggie Mae.

She must be so afraid with all the noise and confusion in the shelter.

The staff is being wonderful to her. They even put her bed in a closet so that she would have a quiet place, but that can't last for long.

Surely somebody will take her?

I scanned the messages for a rescue offer. None had appeared. Somebody needed to get her—and fast. I looked down at my two old Labs, Moody and Siggy, lying next to me on the floor.

"What do you think, boys? Shall we save this damsel in distress?"

They raised their heads to look at me, with a "Whatever" expression in their eyes. They'd hosted foster dogs before. It would be nothing new.

> *It's a long way from Minneapolis to Fairfax, but if you can get her to us, my rescue will take her.*

The chat line hummed again. Was I asking the impossible? Before long a message appeared that could be just the one we needed.

> *I sold a puppy a year ago to a flight attendant for Northwest Airlines. Maybe she can help us.*

The Dog Angels were watching over Maggie Mae. The flight attendant replied:

> *I'd be honored to accompany Miss Maggie Mae on the Northwest flight from Minneapolis to Washington Dulles, at no charge.*

* * *

Maggie Mae arrived at Dulles like a VIP, her crate rolling into the loading dock on a fork lift with the flight attendant close behind.

"I need to run. I have to get on the return flight to Minneapolis." She turned to go, hesitated, then reached into her bag and pulled out a piece of towel. "I almost forgot to give this to you. It's Maggie Mae's snot rag. You'll need it."

She was gone before I could ask, "Why do I need a snot rag?"

I turned to the crate. The forklift driver had left and there was no one else in the cargo area.

"Well, my dear, I guess it's just you and me." I squatted in front of the crate, lifted the latch and started to crack open the door.

Maggie Mae smelled freedom. She blasted out of the crate like a furry rocket, knocking me onto my back. As she flew by I managed to grab one of her hind legs, gripping it like a drowning woman, terrified she might get lost in the depths of Dulles Airport.

Still holding her leg, I struggled to my knees and swung my free arm around her body. She squirmed with all her strength, but once my arms were around her, she calmed enough for me to put on her collar and leash. My heartbeat returned to normal.

"Yikes, Maggie Mae. You gave me a serious scare!"

We made our way to my car, Maggie Mae stepping carefully over the sidewalk she couldn't see.

"Here, let me show you how to get in the car."

With a boost from me, she jumped up and settled on the seat. That's when I saw two large globs of greenish-yellow mucous oozing from her nostrils. She noticed them too. She shook her head. Two globs of mucous slid down the inside of the car window.

"Now I know what the snot rag is for."

* * *

My veterinarian was firm. "You have to keep her separate from your dogs. We don't know what kind of infection she has, and you don't want them all to be sick."

"Okay. Maggie Mae will be on the bottom floor, and the boys will be on the main floor. There's a gate. That should work."

The next day there was a noise from the stairs. Maggie Mae howled, suspended between the two floors, four legs flailing the air. Only her belly held her in place, tightly wedged between the spindles of the stair rail.

"Let me get you out of there, you silly girl. You don't like being alone downstairs, do you?"

As soon as I freed her, she ran to be with the boys. The quarantine was over before it began.

That night Maggie Mae snuggled with the boys on my bed, ignoring the large L.L. Bean dog bed that had been sent by one of the chat line members. But in the morning, when the boys ran down the stairs to get their breakfast, Maggie Mae would not budge from the top step. Nothing could lure her down—not dog biscuits, or chicken, or my offer to help her, one step at a time. She wailed like a child.

I'm so afraid to do this!

"Maggie Mae, you're too heavy for me to carry. You'll just have to wait until I feed the boys, and then we'll see what I can figure out." As I dished out the dog food in the kitchen, I heard a noise behind me. Maggie Mae had conquered her fear, and come down the stairs all by herself.

I started to call her "Maggie Mae the Wonder Dog." Her courage and determination were an inspiration to me. She reminded me of the old Ginger Rogers saying: She could do everything the boys could do—not backwards and in high heels, of course, but without her sight.

* * *

After a couple of months Maggie Mae's sinus infection was cured, and she was ready to go to her forever home. Her adopter arrived in his pick-up to take her away. He knew that I hated to see her go. She had become a part of our family.

"Don't worry about her, Barbara. We have a vacation house on a lake, and a boat, and she will go everywhere with us. She's going to have a great life."

He helped her onto the front seat of his truck and they drove off, Maggie Mae looking straight ahead as if she could already see the good times to come. Her journey from Minnesota was about to have a happy ending in Maryland.

It was hard to say good-bye, but Maggie Mae made sure I would remember her: years after she went on to her new life, I was still finding her snot on my walls and ceiling.

PYGMALION REDUX

Progress is impossible without change, and those who cannot change their minds cannot change anything.

George Bernard Shaw

Her name was Norma Newmark. She was a New York City intellectual. She played tennis with Leonard Bernstein. When she walked into a room, everyone knew she had arrived.

I was in awe of her.

Norma chaired the department at Lehman College of the City University of New York where I went for my Master's degree in 1970. She was a devout feminist and family sociologist. Most of her students were experienced teachers from New York City public schools. Battle-hardened. Blasé. They had seen it all.

I was a housewife from the suburbs who hadn't seen much of anything. My life was defined by the *Ladies' Home Journal* and *Good Housekeeping*. I took pride in keeping the cookie jar full of homemade cookies.

It didn't take long for Norma to seize on my lack of sophistication. She must have been horrified by my domestic persona. But she also must have sensed that somewhere inside me was the potential to grow and change—even if I didn't know it.

Without telling me, she became my mentor. She would be the one to drag me—willing or not—into the real world.

Norma didn't waste any time getting started. She called me to the front of the class to read a list of words.

"Barbara, you need to get used to these words so that you don't look shocked when people say them."

My mother would have called them "dirty words" and probably would have threatened to wash my mouth out with soap. I had never heard them spoken aloud, although I remembered my father saying "hell" once at dinner, shocking the family into silence.

"Go ahead, Barbara. Nice and loud."

I swallowed hard and read the list. The other women in the class laughed. They were in on the joke.

But learning not to blush at profanity was just the first step in Norma's plan. Next came her required class on Human Sexuality.

"Your final grade will be based on the term paper. I'm assigning the topics. Nancy, you'll be writing on *Gender Issues;* Louise, *Values and Attitudes.*"

"And Barbara, your topic is *Female Masturbation.*"

Norma had struck again.

Returning to college almost 20 years after my undergraduate days was like finding myself in a time warp. Congress had just passed the Equal Rights Amendment. Feminists had staged a sit-in at my beloved *Ladies Home Journal,* demanding changes in its "*Feminine Mystique* propaganda." Everyone seemed to be talking about new roles for women.

Norma never stopped prodding me. She invited me to her parties, eclectic mixes of academics, politicians, African Americans, gays, and feminists. I talked with people who challenged me with different views and opinions.

They made me think.

My views began to change. Even my behavior changed. I shocked my female friends by arguing politics with their husbands at our suburban dinner parties. It was then that I adopted my first yellow Labrador and named her Libby in honor of women's lib.

When I finished my degree, Norma asked me to stay on as a member of the faculty. I was to be the department generalist, teaching any class that needed an instructor.

"Barbara, this semester I want you to teach two sections of Child Development."

"Norma, I don't know anything about Child Development."

"You have children, don't you?"

"Yes, I have two."

"That will do."

I taught Child Development for three years, spending much of my time in the housing projects of the South Bronx where my students worked in day care centers for their practical experience.

"Remember to use the elevators, even if they don't smell very good. The addicts shoot up in the stairwells."

Norma had my back.

Working in the projects was a major life event for me. I watched mothers trying to keep their young children safe on the city streets and thought of my comfortable home in the suburbs, with its big yard and swing set.

The projects appeared to house only Hispanics and African Americans. But on warm, sunny days, the benches in the park were filled with another minority—elderly Jews, holding their canes or leaning on their walkers.

I thought: "There must be better housing for poor families with young children. There must be better ways to house the elderly." I was beginning to view the world as a sociologist.

Norma had more projects for me.

"There's a mayor's luncheon at the Waldorf Astoria. I want you to go and represent me."

"There's a tour of the designer workshops on Seventh Avenue. Some big names. Bill Blass for one. You need to see that."

"Take the subway. I know you've never done it before, but you'll figure it out."

Norma pushed me to see and experience it all. I was on a crash course to liberation—exhilarating, frustrating, and a little scary.

* * *

"Come into my office. We need to talk."

Norma's requests were never ignored.

"You really like college teaching, don't you?"

"Yes. I like it a lot. I love working with these kids."

"You will never get anywhere in college teaching without a PhD. You need that. Find a place to get your PhD, and go do it."

"I know what I want to do, Norma. The projects have had such an impact on me. I'm going to study housing sociology."

Norma had done her job. She opened my eyes to the modern world with all of its diversity and excitement. She prepared me to move on. She had successfully transformed her protégé.

I was ready for the next chapter.

* * *

Years later, when a beautiful yellow Lab named Hope came into my life, I thought of Norma and her efforts to shape me into the woman I had become.

Hope: the feisty determined dog who was newly liberated from her life of service as a backyard breeder. Norma would have loved her spirit.

Would I be able to lead Hope into her new life, as Norma had led me?

Hope and I were about to embark on a new adventure, not unlike the one that Norma and I had shared so many years before. And Hope would make that adventure a memorable one.

DISCOVERING HOPE

All of my dogs have been scamps and thieves and troublemakers and I've adored them all.

Helen Hayes

She sat looking out the window of the rescue transport—erect, almost defiant. There was none of the submissive slump of some rescue dogs. Her body language said it all:

Bring it on. I'm ready for what comes next.

She had been a backyard breeder. I pictured her chained to a doghouse, producing puppies for people who hoped to profit from them. Most likely her puppies were sold before she weaned them. In her doggie way, she must have felt the loss. But she had no choice. She was a breeding bitch.

Now, at the age of eight, she was no longer useful. Her owners left her at the county shelter. The surrender papers told the story: "We don't want her anymore."

Hope's life might have ended at the shelter, the fate of many senior dogs. But her luck changed. A dog lover saw her and called Lab Rescue.

"There is a beautiful yellow Lab at the Howard County Shelter. Please save her."

Destiny brought us together when Lab Rescue said, "Yes." I liberated Hope from the shelter, and brought her home to stay with me until she was adopted. It was the beginning of her new life.

* * *

My three Labs, Raleigh, Cody and Maddie, were waiting at home to welcome Hope. They greeted her at the door with curious noses, eager to check her over from head to tail. In no time they blended into one big happy family. At least that's what I thought. But I soon realized that some kind of unseen canine mind meld had taken place. As soon as she arrived, Hope had sent a silent message to the other dogs:

> I am in charge here.

Hope never growled or snapped at another dog. She appeared to be sweetness personified. But no dog ever took Hope's bone or challenged her right to be on the couch. Only Hope came into the room where dog meals were prepared. Somehow, everyone else knew that they had to wait outside. I could almost hear Hope saying:

I took care of that, didn't I?

I whispered to myself, "You go girl."

Hope was my canine alter ego.

* * *

Hope had a potential adopter. Diane was a cancer survivor who had lost her voice, and could only speak through a synthesizer. Her old dog had died, and she was looking for a new Lab. Hope might be the one.

"I've been told that dogs can't hear the synthesizer. I need to spend some time with Hope to see if we can figure out a way to communicate."

Diane sat on my living room floor to be close to Hope. Neither dog nor human had the power of speech. They needed to find their own common language. She took the synthesizer from the chain around her neck and held it to her throat.

"Hi Hope. I'm Diane. Would you like me to pet you?"

The voice was guttural and metallic—much like the sound of an old fashioned robot before engineers figured out how to create *Siri's* sweet tones. Hope ignored it.

After a few more unsuccessful attempts, Diane dropped the synthesizer and started to clap her hands, whistle, and smack her lips. Curiosity got the better of Hope. She walked closer to Diane.

Why is this human making such strange noises?

After a long "interview," Diane decided that Hope would do. I packed up Hope's food and meds. Diane took her leash. Hope jumped into her car. She sat straight on the back seat, looking out the window. She seemed happy to go, but I was already regretting her departure.

Half an hour later, my phone rang. The mechanical voice was without emotion, but the message was clear:

"You must come and get Hope. I opened the back door of the car, and she won't get out. She is baring her teeth at me."

I raced to Diane's house. Hope was still sitting in the back seat. When she saw me, she jumped out and walked to my car, waiting to get in.

Well, I took care of that, didn't I?

Hope came home with me that day, and never left.

She still had more surprises for me.

* * *

Nothing edible was safe from Hope. She learned how to open all the drawers and cabinets in the kitchen. And when she ate the contents of the bread drawer for the second time, I knew I had to act. Unfortunately, I didn't act quickly enough.

Just before Christmas, a package wrapped in brown paper appeared on my neighbors' front porch. I put it on a shelf in my kitchen for safekeeping and went off to run errands.

Back home, I opened the front door to a sea of paper and cardboard. Small fragments were scattered everywhere. Four dogs watched me with interest as I crawled around the floor. Like a detective on a case, I was trying to figure out what had happened.

"What was in that box guys? Was it food? Did you eat it?"

Then I saw it. A small fragment of shiny paper: *Sees Dark Chocolates – 3 pounds.*

I did the math in my head. Three pounds of dark chocolate. Four dogs. If each one ate the same amount of chocolate, it wouldn't be too bad. But suppose one dog got more than the others? I couldn't take the chance.

I loaded four dogs into my SUV and headed for the vet.

Dr. Pierce was ready.

"I'll give each one a dose of peroxide. That should make them vomit up the chocolate. They'll be fine. You got them here just in time."

Three dogs vomited—nothing. Hope watched the activity with quiet stoicism. She didn't vomit.

Dr. Pierce turned to Becky, the vet tech.

"Becky, since the peroxide didn't work for Hope, I guess we will have to use the apomorphine."

Becky bent over Hope to put the drug into her eye.

OORK.

Hope disgorged the better part of three pounds of partially digested chocolates all over Becky.

Becky gasped, jumped back, and started to wipe the chocolate from her face and hair.

OORK.

Hope disgorged the remainder of the three pounds onto Becky's shoes.

Well, I took care of that, didn't I?

Hope became a legend at the animal hospital. I will never know how she managed to keep all of those chocolates to herself. Raleigh was the only dog tall enough to reach the package. He must have dropped it on the floor, where Hope took over. She had three partners in crime, but none of them got even a taste of the stolen goods.

* * *

Hope's determined spirit was an inspiration. At the times when her behavior tested my patience the most, when I shook my head in disbelief at what she had done, I couldn't help but whisper to myself:

"You go girl!"

MIA'S LESSON

Those who teach the most about humanity aren't always humans.

Donald L. Hicks

Seventy-two Labrador Retrievers and a potbellied pig.

One of them was named Mia.

She was never mine, but she taught me a lesson in survival.

* * *

The urgent call went out to Lab rescues from North Carolina to Maine:

> *This is the Sussex County Virginia Sheriff's Department. We have raided the farm of an unlicensed breeder and seized 72 Labrador Retrievers and a Vietnamese potbellied pig. They're living in mud and feces. They're malnourished. Some of them are sick. They need help ASAP. Can you help?*

Lab Rescue offered to take thirty-nine dogs. But not the potbellied pig.

* * *

They became known as the "Sussex Labs." In an orgy of dog care, Lab Rescue's veterinary staff bathed, vetted, and gave shots and medications to all thirty-nine. They removed ticks and trimmed toenails. They cleaned ears. They extracted teeth. They tested and treated for heartworm and parasites. And when the dogs were ready, they messaged the volunteers:

"Come and get your foster dog."

I already had too many Labs at my house, but my friends Ted and Jamie offered to help. They had two Labs, a spacious house and a large fenced yard—the perfect setting for a homeless dog in need.

"I wonder if they'll be traumatized?" Jamie mused as we drove to the veterinary hospital. "There's always an element of excitement when you're about to meet a new dog."

"Yes, and sometimes there are some real surprises." I was remembering some of the more problematic dogs we had fostered in the past.

"I read in the local newspaper that they were fed bread and water, and some have broken bones. Not only that, some were kept in crates so small that they couldn't turn around." Jamie's voice wavered in indignation.

We prepared for a heartbreaking scene.

The barn-like space where the dogs were boarded was filled with chicken wire cages. There was a Lab in each one. Some sat quietly, almost in a daze, as if they hadn't quite figured out what was happening. Others jumped and pawed at the chicken wire, filling the cavernous area with loud barks and yelps. One brought me to tears. She huddled in the corner of her cage and shivered with anxiety.

Jamie's designated foster was Mia, a petite chocolate Lab who sat quietly in her cage, watching the activity around her. Unlike many of the other dogs, she didn't show outward signs of trauma. She allowed us to reach through the wire and stroke her head and ears. She sniffed our fingers. She gently took some treats.

Jamie decided the introduction had gone well. She opened the cage and dropped a new collar over Mia's head. Mia froze. Her eyes widened. Her ears drew back. It was clear she wasn't happy about that strange thing around her neck.

"Time to go home, Mia."

Jamie attached a leash to her new collar, but Mia wouldn't move. Tugging, cajoling, and treats had no effect. Mia wasn't going anywhere as long as she was wearing that intolerable accessory. Finally, Jamie picked her up in her arms and carried her to the car.

"We'll have to work on leash walking some other time."

At home and free of the dreaded collar, Mia ran happily around the yard with the other dogs. It didn't take long to see that despite the trauma, or maybe because of it, Mia had a will of her own. When it was time for dinner, she refused to come into the house. Once again, cajoling, tugging, and the offer of treats had no effect. Any attempt to pick her up and bring her inside sent her wildly racing to the far corners of the yard.

Not wanting to upset her any further, Jamie put Mia's food bowl on the patio, outside the glass doors of the family room, where Mia hungrily licked it clean.

When darkness drove the other dogs inside, Mia still could not be enticed into the house.

"OK. You can stay outside, Mia, if you feel safer there. We'll make a bed for you."

Jamie put a large dog crate on the patio, covered it with a tarp, and filled it with old blankets. Mia approved the arrangement. She snuggled into the blankets and settled in for the night.

After a week, Mia came cautiously into the house, but only for food. She slipped just inside the door, emptied her bowl, and quickly ran back outside to her dog crate sanctuary.

* * *

Mia had been living outside in the crate for weeks.

"Mia, I need to wash those blankets. They've been in that crate since you arrived."

Jamie pulled a blanket out of the crate. There was a thud as a rubber dog bone hit the stone patio. She pulled out another blanket. A stuffed alligator and a knotted rope toy joined the bone. By the time she had removed all the blankets, there was a pile of dog toys lying on the patio.

"Well I'll be, Mia. Every time you came into the house for a meal, you must have carried a prize back to your bed. And nobody saw you do it. You've been a stealth dog."

Mia had never known good food or safe shelter or dog toys. There was good food in this house. And soft beds. Most of all, there were strange objects that smelled like dogs and food and humans. They were scattered around the floor. Her doggie brain found comfort in them. Like a toddler with his "binky," Mia had found her security in a stuffed alligator, a rubber dog bone, and a rope chew toy.

* * *

Mia learned to walk on a leash.

She learned that living in a house was good.

I learned that no matter how bad things might seem, if you can find something soft and fuzzy to hug, your heart will start to mend.

And somewhere in Virginia, a rescued Vietnamese potbellied pig no longer shared his turf with seventy-two Labrador Retrievers.

MOLLY'S FOLLIES

What is life but a series of inspired follies? The difficulty is to find them to do. Never lose a chance: it doesn't come every day.

George Bernard Shaw

When I feel like exploring I go to the Big Flea. It always looks as if half the attics in the county have been emptied into one cavernous space, but I know what I'm looking for.

Cut glass is one. I love the weight of it. The look of it. The sparkling facets reflecting light from every angle. But mostly I love it because it reminds me of my grandmother. I think of her every time I hold one of the pieces she gave me many years ago.

There is cut glass in several of the booths. I'm tempted to buy another dish. But I remember that I'm downsizing so my children won't be burdened with a lot of useless stuff when I die.

I walk away from the cut glass.

Blue and white china. My weakness. It is on display everywhere in the market. There has always been room for another piece at my house.

But not today. I'm downsizing. I think of my children.

The blue and white china is left for someone else.

Lab stuff is something else I look for—always in good supply at the Big Flea. Lab prints. Lab art. Lab postcards. Lab figurines.

I see a print that I don't have.

I remind myself that at home there are walls full of Lab art, and a room full of Lab "tchotchkes." I can't make more work for my children.

Reluctantly, I leave the Lab print behind.

I depart the flea market empty-handed. No cut glass. No blue and white china. No Lab stuff. I assure myself, "This is not the time for acquisition."

* * *

At home, I think about the Big Flea and cry. What used to be a pleasant quest for just the right purchase became an exercise in denial. A glimpse into a dreary future. The realization of unwanted separations to come.

I hold my cut glass and wonder. When I am gone, will anyone treasure it as I do? Will anyone think of my grandmother? Or will my cut glass end up at the flea market—just another purchase for someone who admires its sparkle and weight but cares nothing about its history?

The shelves in my house are full of blue and white china. It has no special sentimental value, but it feels comfortable and familiar. It has been part of my décor since I established my own home. I want to live with it as long as I can.

Someday, someone else will want it— if only because it is pretty and blue and white.

I look around my house at the Lab memorabilia on the walls and shelves. I cherish every piece—the portraits, the memorial wall, the Lab Christmas tree. They remind me of the twenty-plus Labs that have shared my life and the many others that have passed through as fosters. Will my Lab things ever mean as much to someone else as they do to me?

Someday a Lab owner or two will probably be glad to have my memorabilia. But only because it is all about Labs. The memories are all mine.

I know that at my age I shouldn't be adding to my collections. But my heart still clings to things that have meaning for me. I'm not ready to let go.

* * *

The automatic lights on my orchid plants penetrate the morning darkness.

I hear Molly stir on her dog bed next to me and feel her warm breath on my cheek. I squeeze my eyes shut so that she doesn't know I'm awake, but it doesn't work. A cool, wet tongue crosses my face.

It's time to get up.

Dogs love routine. Molly knows it well. As soon as she has cleaned her bowl she is at the front door, bouncing on her front feet. I draw the line at thunderstorms and blizzards, but other than that, like the U.S. Postal Service, nothing keeps us from our appointed rounds.

C'mon. C'mon. We can't waste any time. Let's go!

I fasten Molly's harness with a loud snap, and we are out the door.

Walking Molly is like going on a scientific expedition. She explores with her nose to the ground, eagerly sampling all the new scents on the sidewalk and street.

That golden retriever Tyler peed here last night. And the Chihuahua was right behind him.

A bird chirps loudly in the hedge next to us. Molly's attention is drawn upward. She stops, cocks her head, and listens. Her nostrils quiver with excitement.

There's a mockingbird in there. I just know it!

Molly plunges her head into the hedge. I envision a mockingbird sitting calmly on her nest when an enormous brown nose appears. But Molly's exploration is cut short when the male mockingbird dive bombs us and we run to escape his attack.

Crunch! It's a familiar sound that gets my immediate attention.

Oh, wow! Chicken bone!

It is clearly too late to say "Leave it, Molly"—although that command hardly ever works when a chicken bone is involved. I grab Molly's muzzle, open her jaws, and scoop the offending material out of her mouth with my finger.

I knew it was a long shot, but it was worth a try.

We continue down the sidewalk. Molly freezes. She sits. She sees something up ahead.

What is that? I've never seen it before. It's very scary.

We can't go any farther until Molly checks it out. We detour toward the item in question. It is a brightly colored basketball. Molly looks it over, sniffs it, and determines it to be harmless. We can continue.

Is that one of the feral cats over there?

Molly stops and assumes her stalking posture. The cat pays no attention to her. He soon disappears under a car, and Molly, thank goodness, doesn't chase him.

So go our daily walks. Molly assesses scents on the ground and in the air. She checks out any unfamiliar items on our route, stalks the occasional feral cat, and greets any passing humans who are interested in paying attention to her. The neighborhood is her flea market.

When we get home, she curls up on the couch and is sound asleep in seconds.

* * *

My walks with Molly are more than expeditions. They are Molly's lessons for living.

She is an old lady. Her body is distorted from the puppies she produced as a backyard breeder. Her first eight years were probably spent chained or in a cage. She has scars whose source we will never know.

Yet she savors every walk as if it is the first. It doesn't matter if the weather is bad. It doesn't matter what she encounters along the way. Everything is new and fascinating. She is happy. She lives in the moment.

Molly reminds me that I can live like that, too. I can see a new world every day. I can take joy in the smallest things that cross my path.

Next time I go to the Big Flea, I'm going to buy something for myself. Maybe a piece of cut glass.

My children can deal with it after I'm gone.

LEFT BEHIND

Dogs, for a reason that can only be described as divine, have the ability to forgive, let go of the past, and live each day joyously. It's something the rest of us strive for.

Jennifer Skiff

Midnight. I lie on a thin bare mattress on the floor of a windowless room. The attendant has locked the door and left, his footsteps echoing down the empty hall. There is no escape from the quiet room at Dominion Hospital.

Anger consumes me. Bile rises in my throat. I want to throw something. Or break something. But there is nothing to throw. There is nothing to break.

I can only rip the bandages from my wrists so that my wounds are exposed—bloody and jagged. The torn remnants rest on the floor where I tossed them, silent symbols of my despair.

The attendant has given me some medicine. Sleep will come soon. But not before I remember why I am here.

"Let's not see each other so often. I want to be free to take beautiful women out for dinner." From the man who was supposed to be the love of my life.

A mentally strong woman would have said, "Screw you," and moved on.

But I am not a mentally strong woman.

* * *

Quincy lived in a machine shop in Maryland. I imagine him lying on a filthy dog bed in a corner of the shop, rarely getting a glimpse of the outside world. He ate when someone remembered to feed him. No one paid much attention to him. They were too busy working.

One day the owner closed the shop for good. He silenced the machines, turned off the lights, and bolted the doors. Everyone left. Everyone but Quincy.

By the time Animal Control found Quincy, his big body was skin and bones. He was near death. The volunteer who checked him into the shelter crouched and put her arms around him. She ran her hands over his emaciated body and cried.

"You poor, sweet boy! What terrible things have happened to you? You're safe now. I'm going to take care of you."

Quincy had found his guardian angel. She sat in his run for hours every day to pet him, talk to him, and feed him. She made sure the shelter gave him the veterinary care that he needed.

Quincy's ordeal wasn't over. Animal Control wanted to charge the shop owner for animal abuse. Quincy was evidence. He had to stay at the shelter while Animal Control looked for the owner. They searched for weeks, but never found him. Finally, they dropped the case and Quincy was free to be adopted.

His guardian knew just where she wanted him to go. She contacted Lab Rescue.

"There's a wonderful, big yellow boy here in the shelter. Please take him."

"We don't think he is Lab enough. He doesn't have Lab ears."

"But the rest of him is Lab. He's a great dog."

"We don't usually take dogs with ears like that."

"This dog is special. He has suffered so much, yet he's gentle and loving. I know you'll find him a good home." Quincy's benefactor wouldn't give up until she persuaded the rescue to take him.

Finally, non-Lab ears and all, Lab Rescue agreed to take Quincy. His guardian angel rejoiced. He was ready for a foster home.

* * *

I had four Labs at the time and was pushing my luck with the homeowner association. But nothing could have kept me from adding Quincy to my pack. I couldn't ignore him. He broke my heart.

Quincy's bony skeleton was still much too visible. I fed him puppy food and boiled chicken and extra treats—anything that would help him gain weight. I gave him pain medications and acupuncture and laser treatments for his bad back. I brushed his matted yellow fur until it was smooth and soft.

I took Quincy to my veterinary surgeon to see if more could be done for his back. Dr. Bradley examined Quincy's spine and legs with his skilled hands. He manipulated Quincy's hips and stroked his head.

He put his hand on my arm:

"You are doing all the right things for Quincy. Take him home and care for him as you have been. There is nothing more to do."

I knew the meaning of Dr. Bradley's unspoken words. Quincy would never fully recover. He would live the rest of his life with me.

As Quincy regained his health, he began to enjoy the company of the other dogs. His benefactor was right. He was gentle and loving. He was even finding that humans could be good. He was learning to trust.

And then one night when I was sitting on the couch, Quincy put his head in my lap and looked up at me.

I need some loving!

My eyes filled with tears. This dog who suffered so much at the hands of humans had come to me for affection. I scratched his ears and rubbed his muzzle. When he decided it was enough, he dropped to the floor and went to sleep at my feet.

It became our special ritual. Whenever I sat on the couch, Quincy put his head in my lap, and looked up at me.

I need some loving!

He always got what he needed.

Then he went to sleep on the floor beside me, trusting that he would never be abandoned again.

* * *

Hope was on the floor, contentedly grinding away at her bone. All the dogs knew that she was not to be disturbed when she was in the "bone zone."

But not Quincy. Either he hadn't gotten the message, or he had chosen to ignore it. He lay next to Hope, his body against hers, his head next to her head—like two spoons in a drawer. If Hope noticed he was there, she gave no indication of it. For several minutes, Hope chewed while Quincy dozed.

I watched, poised to intervene. I was sure this would not end happily.

Suddenly, Quincy swung his head and snatched Hope's bone from her mouth. Hope's eyes opened wide. She looked at me with an amazed expression on her face.

Did you see what he did?

Quincy had just done the unthinkable. But Hope didn't react. She even stayed next to Quincy while he chewed her bone. Sweet gentle Quincy had managed to captivate even Hope, the dog who was always in charge and whose bone should never be stolen. It was a historic moment in the annals of the Osgood dogs.

* * *

Psychiatrists have explained why fear of abandonment became a part of my damaged psyche. It is good to understand. But there is nothing to be gained from revisiting the past.

Quincy showed me how to survive abandonment. He was neglected. He nearly died. Yet he lived through the ordeal to become a gentle loving dog. He learned to forgive humans. He trusted the human who cared for him, and asked for love.

I would like to be more like Quincy.

I would like to be able to trust.

Maybe then, like Quincy, I can overcome abandonment with love.

SOUL SEARCHING

Folk will know how large your soul is, by the way you treat a dog.

Charles F. Duran

Chucho. Raleigh. Zoe.

Three rescued Labs whose journey took them from the shelter to the top of a mountain in Haymarket, Virginia.

* * *

Chucho, my new foster Lab, bounded into the yard. His nose told him there were other dogs nearby. He searched the yard for them, his tail wagging in anticipation.

The middle-aged couple who brought Chucho from the shelter lingered long enough to tell me what they knew about him.

"He's very lively and he's insanely crazy about tennis balls."

"Yes, and our friends are telling us his name means Christ in Spanish. That wouldn't be good, would it? We couldn't keep a name like that, could we?"

It was clear they were much more concerned about Christ than tennis balls.

"Don't worry. I'll check it out. I'm sure I can find someone who can tell me what Chucho means in Spanish."

It didn't take long to find out that Chucho means *mutt* in Central America. I imagined Chucho's Salvadoran owner enjoying the joke as he decided on a name for his handsome chocolate Lab. The rescue would be pleased to know Chucho's name was safe.

Chucho's transporters might have been unduly worried about his name, but they were right on when it came to tennis balls. Chucho's world revolved around them. As long as I threw, Chucho chased, grabbing the adored yellow orb in his teeth, and dropping it at my feet for another round.

At night, I hid the tennis balls where he couldn't find them. Or at least I tried. If he knew where they were, he whined and barked. Like a clumsy magician, I had to find another place to make them disappear when he wasn't looking.

Chucho had to go to a home where there would always be tennis balls. I knew the perfect place. My friend Larry had retired from the white-shirt executive offices of IBM to his ten acre dream home on top of a mountain. He had cleared trees and brush from around the house for an open space to throw tennis balls for his Labs. He was fully equipped with buckets of balls and an ergonomic tennis ball hurler.

Chucho and Larry belonged together.

A few days later, Chucho jumped into my SUV and we headed for the mountain. Larry waited in the yard with his Labs, a supply of the treasured balls, and his handy hurler.

Chucho was in tennis ball heaven.

He didn't even notice when I got in the car and drove away.

Even though he had only been with me for a week, I knew I would miss Chucho and his passion. I always missed my foster dogs. I fussed over them like an anxious mother. Did they go to the right home? Were they getting proper care? Were they loved?

Chucho had found his forever home.

* * *

There was no middle-aged couple to transport Raleigh from the shelter to my house. His journey to the top of the mountain took a different route, beginning with the couple who had adopted him.

> *Dear Lab Rescue:*
>
> *We fell in love with Raleigh the minute we saw him at the shelter. The other dogs were barking*

and yelping, and he just sat there. My husband said he looked like some rich guy who was hoping for better days.

When we took him home, though, we found out he didn't know very much at all. He needed house training and leash training. He had to be taught how to go up and down stairs and through doorways. He cowered as soon as my husband shifted the car into forward gear and gunned the engine. We don't think Raleigh has ever lived in a house or ridden in a car.

Unfortunately, we can teach Raleigh to go up and down stairs, but we can't teach him to love the animals on our farm. His favorite prey are the chickens that range around our barn. I've spent hours sitting in the chicken coop with him in an attempt to establish a truce, but I'm afraid the situation is hopeless.

Sadly, we have come to the conclusion that we can't provide the kind of home Raleigh deserves. We feel that the best thing for Raleigh is for him to be rehomed. He is a very loving dog, just not suited for our lifestyle, which makes him miserable.

I hope you can help.

Raleigh's adopters

* * *

Raleigh needed a new home right away. Maybe a home on top of a mountain. A home that loves Labs. A home that has flocks of tennis balls, but no flocks of chickens.

Raleigh was going to Larry's house.

* * *

My new foster from the shelter was a little chocolate Lab named Zoe. She was the female version of Chucho—another tennis ball addict.

Zoe's zeal for chasing tennis balls was exceeded only by her ability to find them where they had been hidden. One day I hid the tennis ball high up on my bookcase. Zoe knew it was there. She pranced and barked in frustration, like a toddler having a tantrum. Suddenly she was quiet. She had another idea. She selected a videotape from a lower shelf and brought it to me:

> If we can't throw a tennis ball, can we maybe throw this?

The only time Zoe wasn't thinking about tennis balls was when she was sleeping. And, for all I know, she was dreaming about them too.

Like Chucho, Zoe needed to go to a place where there were lots of tennis balls and somebody willing to throw them.

Could I persuade Larry to take another Lab?

* * *

Zoe and I took the familiar route to Larry's. Past the lush green fields where Black Angus grazed. Up the rocky narrow road to the top of the mountain.

Larry and his Labs—Chucho, Raleigh, and Oliver—were waiting in the driveway to greet us.

Raleigh ignored Zoe as if he already knew they didn't have anything in common. He wandered around the yard, checking for new scents. While he might have loved chasing chickens, Raleigh had no interest in tennis balls. He was content just to be where the action was.

Oliver was too old to chase anything. His rotund figure was a tribute to Larry's good cooking. He just sat and watched.

But Zoe and Chucho became instant tennis ball buddies. Larry hurled, and they ran, falling over each other in their enthusiasm. They didn't seem to mind who got the ball. The thrill was in the chase. Finally they collapsed, panting, on the lawn.

Larry gave each of the dogs one of his homemade dog bones and we headed into the house for a glass of wine. We both knew the purpose of my visit, but, like a good salesman, I was waiting for the right moment to close.

"Well, Larry, what do you think? Would you like to keep Zoe?"

Larry didn't hesitate. He'd been waiting all afternoon to deliver his punch line.

"If you'll take Raleigh, I'll keep Zoe."

And that's how Raleigh came to my house, the last stop on his journey to a better life.

RALEIGH'S REMEDY

Thorns may hurt you, men desert you, sunlight turn to fog; but you're never friendless ever, if you have a dog.

Douglas Malloch

The pale hulk of a man struggled up the path to the shopping center, swaying from side to side as if his legs couldn't bear the full weight of his body. His oversize T-shirt hung askew, exposing a bare shoulder. He bent his shaved head toward the ground in an unspoken message:

Leave me alone!

Raleigh and I often met him on our daily walks along the same path. I wasn't surprised by his lack of communication. He lived in the neighborhood halfway house for men recovering from mental illness. Still, I thought T-shirt Man might be afraid of a large black dog like Raleigh. I shortened Raleigh's leash and pulled him close to me, as the man and I passed without speaking.

One day I noticed T-shirt Man on a bench in front of Walmart. He sat hunched over his knees with his eyes to the ground, oblivious to the people coming and going around him. But the man next to him was as talkative as T-shirt Man was taciturn. He called to me as I passed:

"What a great-looking dog! Can I pet him?"

"Yes, he loves the attention."

Raleigh was the strong silent type, but few could resist his soulful brown eyes. He stood quietly while the man patted his head and scratched his ears.

"He has a gray muzzle. Is he old?"

"Yes, he's a senior citizen as dogs go. He's eleven years old."

"I suppose he has arthritis, just like I do. Seems to me there is something they give dogs for that. I'm not sure what it's called."

"Glucosamine."

Not only the correct answer, but the first word I had ever heard T-shirt Man utter.

"It's called Glucosamine." He repeated it, as if we might not have heard him the first time.

I turned to T-Shirt Man, who had now raised his head and was looking at Raleigh. "You must be a dog lover. Not everyone knows about glucosamine."

"I had a dog a long time ago. She had arthritis. That's what I gave her."

"I have to apologize, then. I thought you might be afraid of a large black dog. That's why I always held him back from you."

"No, I'm not afraid of dogs." He reached out to pet Raleigh. "Did you say his name is Raleigh?"

"Yes. And what is yours?"

"I'm Brian."

When we met on the path after that, Brian always stopped to pet Raleigh. While he scratched Raleigh's ears, I learned more about him. Like me, he suffered from bipolar disorder. But unlike me, he hadn't found a treatment that helped. He couldn't work, and was living on disability. We talked about his struggles, his family, and his past. We talked about dogs.

A year after we met, Brian relapsed and had to return to the hospital. We never saw him again.

I miss him—that giant of a man who suffered so much, but always had a gentle touch for Raleigh. I still watch for him in the hope that someday he'll come lumbering down the path, his white T-shirt flapping in the wind, a smile on his face. A smile that tells me he has found a cure.

* * *

The bearded man sat on a bench in the mini-park next to the bus stop. Raleigh and I passed him every day. He smoked cigarettes and drank coffee from a Styrofoam cup, a quiet presence amid the turmoil of the shopping center. But one day there was no coffee or cigarette. The man hunched in the pouring rain, wrapped in a poncho and holding a broken umbrella over his head. I called the police.

"This isn't a complaint, but there's a man sitting on a bench in the rain at the shopping center. Could you just check on him and make sure he's Okay?"

Minutes later an officer called: "We've talked to him. He's fine. He's a homeless man, but he doesn't want us to take him to a shelter. He prefers to stay where he is."

A homeless man? In my suburban shopping center?

I began waving to the man every time Raleigh and I walked by. He waved back.

Then one day I moved toward him, holding Raleigh close. "Do you like dogs?"

"Sure."

"Would you like to meet Raleigh?"

"Sure."

And that's how Raleigh and I met Cecil.

Visiting with Cecil became part of our daily walk. I brought extra dog biscuits for Cecil to give Raleigh, who took them gently from his fingers. We sat on the bench together and, while Cecil petted Raleigh and fed him treats, he told me his life story.

That autumn, the weather turned suddenly cold. I worried about Cecil. I knew that he slept on the ground, rolled up in a poncho. But would that keep him warm enough? I ran to the nearest sporting goods store for a couple of space blankets. It was dark by the time I got to Cecil with the packages, but he was still in his usual place.

"Cecil, it's going to be very cold tonight. I hope these will help to keep you warm. It's the best I could do on short notice."

Cecil took the packages. "What do we have here?"

He held the plastic wrappers close to his face. He turned them sideways and upside down. He fumbled with the flaps.

"What did you give me?"

That's when I discovered that Cecil was nearly blind.

It was Cecil's good fortune to be homeless in our shopping center. He had a large support system—a man who drove by every Saturday to give him cash, a woman who bought him a new back pack, local police officers who brought fast food, managers of the gas station who allowed him to use their restroom. We joked that people brought so many Thanksgiving dinners he couldn't eat them all.

His supporters rushed to do something about Cecil's eyesight. We made phone calls. We wrote letters. We filled binders with paperwork for Social Security and Medicaid. We worked with non-profit groups that support the homeless.

It took many months, but Cecil got his medical evaluation. Good news. He wasn't permanently blind. He had severe cataracts, but once they were removed, he would have normal vision. Surgery completed, Cecil was a new man.

The last time Raleigh and I saw Cecil, we sat together once again on the bench in the shopping center. He was full of enthusiasm for the future. He was going to get a job. He would find an apartment. He looked at me:

"You're a blonde. I always thought you had black hair." We laughed.

Cecil and I shook hands. He patted Raleigh's head. We said "Good-bye." Cecil was on his way to a new life.

* * *

Brian and Cecil were Raleigh's special friends. But he also had a larger fan club. Like a local politician, he trotted the length of the shopping center, stopping along the way to meet and greet his "public."

There was Oscar, who worked at Target and took his break in front of the store so that he could give Raleigh a treat. There was the man we called Sushi Man, who drank his morning coffee on the empty patio of the sushi restaurant where we stopped to say "Good morning" and talk about the weather.

For the holiday season, Raleigh sported a large red bow on his harness. People smiled when they saw him, even if they didn't stop to talk. And Raleigh's biggest fan, the manager of the Hallmark store, gave him a Christmas gift of red and green tennis balls.

* * *

To Raleigh, everyone was a friend. He drew me to people I might not have spoken to without him. Friendship. It was Raleigh's remedy for the blues.

LIFE AND DEATH

There is a land of the living and a land of the dead, and the bridge is love, the only survival, the only meaning.

Thornton Wilder

A nurse gasped.

The hospital delivery room fell silent.

Dr. Rooney's voice sounded strange and distant. "Bad news, Mrs. Osgood. Your baby isn't going to live."

I felt the wheels of my gurney turn as an orderly pushed me out of the gleaming white space, down the hall and into an empty room. He left without speaking, closing the door behind him.

I lay motionless under the stiff white sheets. How could this be? Dr. Rooney had heard the baby's heart only minutes earlier. I had felt him kick for weeks.

No one could have known that the child we named David would not survive outside his mother's womb. In 1962 there was no amniocentesis; no ultrasound. No one knew that David was missing part of his brain and skull.

I heard nurses whispering outside my door. "Has she cried yet?"

Cry? My body and mind were floating in a sea of nothingness. I couldn't cry.

The sounds of maternity were all around me—muffled conversations, babies crying, the squeaking wheels of gurneys and food carts. But my room was without sound or light. My body was frozen in place, as if any movement might cause it to splinter and disappear into the void.

A nurse came into the room and stood by my bed. She took my hand. "Your baby had broad shoulders. He would have been a big boy. We put him in a bassinet in the back of the nursery. There was nothing we could do for him. He died a few minutes ago."

She squeezed my hand and left, leaving me alone in the silent room.

David had lived for two hours, alone and untouched. I never saw him. I never held him. No one asked me if I wanted to.

Overwhelming sadness followed me home the next day—to the empty bedroom with its circus train wallpaper, the crib with its animal-patterned sheets, and the dresser full of carefully folded baby clothes. Painful reminders that the child for whom it all was intended was never coming home.

No one suggested a funeral. My family was anxious to put this event behind them as quickly as possible. They did not deal well with grief.

My husband buried his feelings in logistics. "I know an undertaker who has a baby casket in stock. We can bury David right away in the family cemetery plot."

He struggled to understand my emotions: "How could you possibly be so upset about a baby you never saw?"

But I was. For a long time. Maybe forever.

Never again would someone I love die alone.

* * *

This, I realized, is how we learn about grief. No one can teach us about it. Nothing can prepare us for it. When grief comes into our lives, we must find our own way to make sense of it, to overcome it and move on.

When I lost David, I needed someone to hold me. To weep with me. To feel my pain.

It didn't happen.

So I found my own way to deal with grief. Alone. Deep inside. A communication between my mind and heart that is shared with no one. No less painful or intense because I hide it from view.

* * *

"It's cancer. Osteosarcoma. The laboratory analysis says it has probably metastasized."

Dr. Taylor had removed a mass from Raleigh's dew claw. While I waited for the lab report, I prayed that it would be benign. I wasn't ready to say good-bye to another dog. But Dr. Taylor had bad news.

It was just a matter of time.

This wasn't my first experience with canine cancer. I wasn't going to give up without a fight. I scoured the Internet for new treatments and found promising research on the use of Chinese mushrooms. I ordered the large capsules and fed the maximum amount to Raleigh every day. Just doing it gave me hope. Maybe we could beat this dreaded disease.

After the surgery, Raleigh was his old self. He loved to walk, and once his leg was healed we went back to greeting his friends in the shopping center. Months went by, and I began to convince myself we had escaped. Maybe the mushrooms had worked after all.

Then Raleigh started to cough during the night. We made another trip to the vet. I watched the computer image while Dr. Taylor used the ultrasound to check him. "It's the cancer. You can see the fluid that is starting to accumulate in his lungs. I'll give you some medication that will help."

When Raleigh woke up coughing, I gave him his pain pills. I lay beside him on the floor, my arms around his big chest, until the medicine took effect. I could feel his body relax and his breathing grow soft and regular. When I knew he was asleep and free from pain, I could sleep too.

One night the coughing was different, more intense. I gave Raleigh his medicine but it didn't help. I tried to hold him, but his body twisted and flailed. He was suffering. I knew it was time to make our final journey to the emergency vet.

"We can try to work on him and see what we can do to help him. Would you like that?" The vet wanted me to make the decision.

"No. Raleigh has told me it's time to go. I don't want him to suffer any longer. We knew this day was coming."

I hugged his body close to me and whispered in his ear, "I love you, buddy. You have been my best boy. I will always love you."

I wanted my voice to be the last sound he heard.

"Good boy, Raleigh. Good boy. Good boy. . . ."

Until the vet told me his heart had stopped.

* * *

Raleigh was gone. I felt spent, empty. I drove home, buried my face in Daffy's soft yellow fur and cried.

"Raleigh's gone, Daffy. He's gone to the Rainbow Bridge. But our other dogs are there to greet him. He isn't sick any more. He's happy."

Daffy lifted her head and licked the salty tears from my face.

AWAKENING

Until one has loved an animal, a part of one's soul remains unawakened.

Anatole France

He was tall and handsome.

His hair was the color of amber honey.

His appeal was magnetic.

His name was Cody.

It was love at first sight.

* * *

I brought my SUV to a stop in an empty space at the Exxon station just off Route 95. Rain pounded on the roof and streamed down the windshield. I leaned back in my seat and waited, watching a raindrop make its crooked path down the window.

A printed e-mail lay on the seat beside me:

> *The transport will arrive around 3:00 pm. Your new foster dog will be on board, He is an 11-year-old male named Cody. He was a stray to the shelter, so we don't know any more about him. He is a nice dog, though.*

I had barely opened the book I brought to pass the time when another SUV parked next to me. A casual observer might have suspected clandestine activity. I knew it was my special delivery.

Through the rain I could see a big Lab sitting on the back seat. He was a good-looking fox-red boy. He turned his head and looked at me. His sad brown eyes met mine. I felt a lump in my throat.

Where have you been Cody? Such a beautiful boy! Who could have given you up to the shelter? Or lost you and never come looking for you?

By the time we had transferred Cody to my car, I knew that he would never be a foster. "He's coming to me," I told the transport driver. "He is going to be mine."

* * *

Cody was going home to meet my three other dogs: Hope, the assertive female; Maddie, the quiet one; and Raleigh, the big old boy.

"Well, Cody" I counselled him on the ride home. "I hope you will be able to blend into this crazy family."

He did. Except for one thing.

The bed.

My tall four-poster bed was hallowed ground. Raleigh was the only dog who could jump high enough to reach it. Hope and Maddie were content to sleep on the floor next to it, but Raleigh always slept on the bed.

When Cody arrived, he wanted to sleep on the bed, too. But he couldn't jump like Raleigh. He stood on his hind legs and put his front paws on the edge of the mattress. His brown eyes pleaded.

Give me a boost—please?

Every night, Raleigh jumped up on the bed. As soon as I boosted Cody, Raleigh jumped off.

"This is silly, guys. It's a queen-size bed. There's room enough for both of you."

I tried to make them lie together. I even tried holding them in place. But there was no way they would both stay on the bed. Finally, a truce. Some nights Raleigh slept on the bed and some nights Cody slept on the bed.

There was probably some profound dog psychology at work here that I never understood. Or perhaps it was an obscure version of dog etiquette. I never knew who would end up on the bed. I only know they made it work without any help from me.

* * *

Cody became the go-to guy whenever Lab Rescue LRCP needed a Lab to meet the public. His poster-dog looks and calm demeanor made him the perfect ambassador. He loved to meet new people, especially children. And he loved to ride in the car.

"There's a Girl Scout troop that's having a program about dogs Can Cody go?"

"Petco is sponsoring a rescue event. Can you bring Cody and set up a booth?"

"Lab Rescue is getting an award. We'd like Cody to be our representative at the presentation."

Cody and I were a team, although I was definitely the supporting member. Cody was the star. He reveled in his stardom. I accepted the supporting role.

Cody was my heart dog.

* * *

Cody developed a lump on his shoulder. Old Labs are prone to tumors under their skin. Most of them are benign lipomas. But some aren't.

I assumed Cody's was benign until my vet removed it and sent it away for biopsy. The news could not have been worse. The growth was a hemangiosarcoma—a virulent form of cancer that had already killed several of my dogs.

I made a decision that I would grow to regret.

"Cody, you aren't going to die of hemangiosarcoma. I'll do anything to keep that from happening. We're going to fight."

*   * *

The oncologist's voice was soft and reassuring with the hint of an accent from his Irish homeland.

"We'll start Cody on doxorubicin—a series of six treatments. It's an intravenous chemotherapy. You'll have to bring him into the hospital so he can spend the night, but he'll be fine. Don't worry. Dogs do much better on chemo than humans do." He grimaced. "They don't lose their hair, for one thing."

Cody tolerated the treatments well, just as Dr. McNeill predicted. But once they were complete, there was more to come.

"We're going to move on to another chemotherapy regimen. It's called Palladia. It's an oral treatment that you can administer yourself."

Dr. McNeill handed me a bottle of little pink pills. They looked like candy. Could they really be powerful enough to fight Cody's cancer?

"You need to handle the pills with surgical gloves. Don't hold them in your bare hands. Your skin will absorb the chemo."

Maybe they were powerful enough to fight cancer after all.

After a few doses, the pills made Cody very ill. He lay motionless on his bed on the patio, staring into space. Even a passing squirrel couldn't excite his attention. I cried as I sat next to him and stroked his head.

Then he stopped eating.

"Cody, you have to eat." Nothing tempted him. Not chicken, or hamburger, or any of his favorite foods.

I was determined to get nourishment into him. I opened his mouth and spooned yogurt onto his tongue. I found a large syringe, and pumped strained baby food between his teeth. I used the syringe to get water into his mouth and down his throat.

My beloved boy was suffering. I called Dr. McNeill.

"It's the Palladia," he said. "You need to stop the treatment."

Cody slowly recovered his appetite and some of his strength. We made a long trip together to visit family in Massachusetts, stopping along the way to satisfy our craving for McDonald's cheeseburgers. Cody tried to be his sociable self, but it was clear that he was failing.

On the way back home, he wouldn't eat his cheeseburger.

I knew that we needed to savor the time we had left.

Days later, I sat on the family-room sofa, reading a book. Rain made quiet puddles on the patio outside my window. Cody lay next to me on his bed. I could hear his measured breathing. And then, suddenly, I couldn't. I slid off the sofa to my knees and bent over him.

"Cody boy. Are you OK?" I stroked his fur and looked into his empty eyes.

Cody was gone. I pulled his lifeless body into my lap and held his head.

My heart dog. My buddy. My friend.

Raindrops made paths down the window, like the tears that fell on amber honey fur.

Buddy

Rescued July 6, 1999
Died October 28, 2002

They will not go quietly, the dogs who've shared our lives,
In subtle ways they let us know their spirit still survives.
Old habits still make us think we hear barking at the door,
Or step back when we drop a tasty morsel on the floor.
Our feet still go around the place the food dish used to be,
And sometimes, coming home at night, we miss them terribly.
And although time may bring new friends
and a new food dish to fill,
That one place in our hearts belongs to them
and always will.

IN MEMORIAM

Soon or late, every dog's master's memory becomes a graveyard, peopled by wistful little furry ghosts that creep back unbidden, at times, to a semblance of their olden lives.

Albert Payson Terhune

The package came in the mail.

It was too big for my mailbox, so Vicky, my mail lady, brought it to the door. Any other day she would have put it on the doorstep and left. That day she rang the bell and waited for me.

"I'm so sorry." Her eyes were filled with tears.

She put the package in my hands, gave me a quick hug, and ran down the steps to her truck.

I carried the brown paper-wrapped bundle into the kitchen and cut the tape that held it together. Inside was a heavy wood box, its plain honey-colored surface shiny with varnish. There were no hinges or latches. I couldn't open it. I didn't need to. I knew what it held.

Buddy's ashes.

* * *

Buddy. My joyful boy. My playboy. The dog that chased tennis balls until he dropped. Moody's and Siggy's playmate. The first of the trio to go to the Rainbow Bridge.

He had been with me for three years when cancer took over his body. I knew he was dying, but I didn't want to give up. I plied the veterinarian with questions.

"What more can we do?"

"Aren't there some other treatments?"

"Should I take him for a consult?"

She shook her head.

"There's nothing more to do. He's suffering. You need to let him go."

The doctor advised, but the decision to say good-bye was mine. In the past there were friends or family to share the burden. Now there was no one to lean on. How could I be sure I was doing the right thing? Who would help me decide?

At home, Buddy, lay curled in the puffy folds of his favorite L.L. Bean bed. I sat on the floor beside him and scratched his ears. I wanted to be close to him, to feel the warmth of his body and the rhythm of his pulse.

Buddy lifted his head and looked at me through clouded eyes that only weeks before had been sparkling and alert. His once joyous personality had been replaced by lethargy. He no longer relished his bowl of kibble and chicken. He had withdrawn into a place inside his head. Even the gentle scratching of his ears couldn't lift his spirits.

> If you listen and look very carefully, I will tell you what I need.

I listened. I looked. And I knew.

Buddy was sharing my burden.

* * *

Buddy lay in my lap. Sedatives made him groggy, but his breathing was slow and effortless. There was no more pain. I stroked his soft yellow fur and whispered to him.

"I love you, Buddy Boy. You're my good friend. We had so much fun. I will miss you."

As I held his head I thought about the day he arrived in the family. The way he had badgered Moody and Siggy to play. The way he had made us laugh at his antics. His joy at the mere sight of a yellow tennis ball.

The veterinarian's voice interrupted my reverie.

"Do you want the ashes?" Her question seemed to come from a different time and place.

"You have a choice. You can have the ashes or leave them at the crematorium."

I didn't want to have this conversation. I wanted to grieve. I wanted to focus on Buddy. We didn't have much more time together.

"Send me the ashes."

It seemed like what a caring responsible dog owner should do.

* * *

Now, a week later, I was holding Buddy's ashes.

I put the box on a shelf in the living room bookcase between a stack of books and a pottery vase I had bought at a craft show in New Hampshire. It looked out of place. I tried another shelf next to the CD player. It didn't look right there either.

The box didn't seem to belong anywhere.

Moody and Siggy watched as I moved it around. I wondered if they knew what was in it.

I moved the box back to its original location, next to the pottery vase. Maybe I would get used to it there.

* * *

Saying goodbye becomes a way of life in a house full of old dogs.

Sometimes it happens much too often.

A year after Buddy died, Moody succumbed to cancer of the spleen. The following year Siggy died from complications of laryngeal paralysis.

Three heavy shiny boxes in three years. They sat in the bookshelf like unwelcome guests. Ugly. Anonymous. They held no meaning for me. No emotion. This was not the way I wanted to remember the trio that had brought me such joy and love.

I wanted to remember my boys as they were: full of life, handsome, loving, and playful. I wanted to remember them with mischievous eyes, wagging tails, and tongues that gave slobbery kisses. I wanted to remember their silly habits that made them special. But how?

Pictures. I had dozens of them. A picture wouldn't be anonymous. It wouldn't be ugly. It would have character and life. It would forever preserve a precious expression, a tail wag, or a cocked ear.

I started with Buddy's happy face—a photo of him lying on the deck in the sun. I added the date that I rescued him and the date he died. I searched my books, files, and the Internet for a quotation that seemed right for him. Then a sympathy card arrived from a friend. It bore a verse that was perfect for Buddy.

BUDDY

Rescued: July 6, 1999

Died: October 28, 2002

They will not go quietly, the dogs who've shared our lives,

In subtle ways they let us know their spirit still survives.

Old habits still make us think we hear barking at the door

Or step back when we drop a tasty morsel on the floor.

Our feet still go around the place the food bowl used to be,

And sometimes, coming home at night, we miss them terribly.

And although time may bring new friends

And a new food dish to fill,

That one place in our hearts belongs to them

And always will.

Pictures of Moody and Siggy followed. I hung all three in the stairwell of my house—a place where I could see them every day. My memorial wall was launched.

Over time, the memorial wall grew. Three frames became five. Then six. And, at last count, nineteen. Nineteen happy Labby faces. Bizzy holding her bowl. Moody surveying his world from the front steps. Cody lying in his favorite chaise on the patio. Hope, posing like a queen. Buddy sunning on the deck.

My furry ghosts surround me. Every time I see them, they bring smiles and memories of the special role each one has played in my life.

* * *

But what to do with the three boxes that were gathering dust in my bookcase? I couldn't throw them away. They were sacred. They held the spirits of Moody, Siggy and Buddy.

One summer weekend I put them in the trunk of my car and drove to my daughter's house in Massachusetts. She is a passionate gardener who is always experimenting with creative and sometimes quirky ideas to enhance her efforts. A fish pond with a waterfall of natural stone. A rose arbor decorated with colored bottles. A flower bed enhanced with a background of mirrors.

Maybe she could find a place for my boxes.

I arrived as she was working on her newest project, a heart-shaped planter decorated with colored stones and small round mirrors.

I lifted the boxes from the car.

"Can we find a place in the woods to scatter these ashes?"

"Not the woods, Mom. Give them to me. They should go here. It's a garden of love."

Buddy's, Moody's, and Siggy's ashes disappeared under the deep rich soil of the heart-shaped planter. They would soon be covered with flowers.

I drove home knowing that my three Labketeers had found their perfect resting place.

And though they might never be seen, three little furry ghosts were standing watch.

FAITHFUL FRIENDS

There are three faithful friends—an old wife, an old dog, and ready money.

Benjamin Franklin

Is there a dog lover alive who doesn't have an arsenal of dog photos?

Like eager new parents, we document our dogs from every angle—eating, sleeping, running, doing silly things. We frame their pictures. We post them on Facebook, YouTube, and Instagram. We save them on our cell phones so that they are available at a moment's notice, whenever the topic of dogs arises.

It is a rare dog owner who can't produce an image of his or her dog on cue.

Proud owners have been immortalizing their dogs for centuries. In the 1700s, they didn't have Facebook or Instagram—or even cameras. They had paintings.

The eighteenth-century artist George Stubbs was one of the first to capture the personalities of dogs on canvas—a barge dog, a spaniel, and a Pomeranian. Other artists of the era reflected the emerging interest in dogs as companions by including them in the portraits of their owners.

* * *

The man stands with his elbow on a split-rail fence with the verdant English countryside in the background. One hand rests in the pocket of his elegant coat, its velvet lapels open wide to display the silver-trimmed waistcoat beneath. His white-stockinged legs are crossed in a casual pose appropriate for a country gentleman. The cravat at his neck is yet another sign that he is man of style and substance.

The long-haired chestnut and white spaniel lying in the grass at his feet gazes up at him in adoration.

The gentleman's name is William Wollaston. Thomas Gainsborough painted his portrait in 1759.

The woman's *robe volante* billows with yards of yellow silk. Her neckline is outlined with a ruffled white panel, held in place with a string of pearls. Lace ruffles are repeated at the edges of her elbow-length sleeves. The panniers that widen her skirt at the hips show that she is a woman of fashion.

Her black and white spotted dog, perhaps a Dalmatian, balances on his hind legs and reaches to place his front paws at her waist. Her hand rests on his head as he extends his neck to look up at her.

The woman's name is Henrietta, Lady Jenkinson. Phillippe Mercier painted her portrait in 1742.

* * *

I have always been fascinated by the eighteenth-century portraits of gentry and their dogs. They were a popular subject for the famous artists of the day—not only Gainsborough and Mercier, but also John Singleton Copley, Joshua Reynolds, William Hogarth, and Pompeo Batoni. Sometimes the dog achieved lasting fame in the title of the painting, as in Batoni's "Sir Harry Fetherstonhaugh with His Faithful Hound," painted in 1776.

It was the Age of Enlightenment, an era when, some claim, people first began to think of their dogs as pets, as animals with feelings and personalities. They displayed devotion to their dogs by having their portraits painted with them.

I have taken dozens of photographs of my dogs. Solo dogs. Dogs in twos and threes and fours. Dogs on sofas, on beds, and in chairs. Dogs in snow, and in the summer flower garden. Sleeping dogs. Walking dogs. Dogs swimming in the surf.

But my favorite pictures are the portraits done by my friend and professional pet photographer, Michael Joseph. Over the past twenty years, Michael has taken many photos for me—some of me with my dogs, some of just the dogs. His portraits are works of art. The finished product looks much like an oil painting.

Eighteenth-century paintings were on my mind one year as I was getting ready for my photo session with Michael. I remembered the portraits of proud men and women, dressed in their most elegant clothes, with their dogs at their feet or in their laps. I remembered the significance of that period in history, when dogs became members of the family for the first time. A time when Benjamin Franklin quipped about "faithful friends" and the poet Alexander Pope wrote, "Histories are more full of examples of fidelity of dogs than of friends."

"Michael, do you know the paintings of people and dogs that were done in the eighteenth century?"

"Sure, I've seen them in the museums, and I have some of them in my art books."

"I want a picture like that."

"You want what?" Michael looked surprised.

"I want a picture of me, all dressed up, with my dogs at my feet, just like a Gainsborough. Can you do that?"

"Of course I can. Bring your gear to the appointment, and we'll make it happen."

I arrived at the appointment with two Labs in one hand, and a garment bag in the other. Nykey, my yellow boy, and Maddie, my chocolate girl, strained at their leashes. They were energized by a ride in the car and a new destination. I hoped we would be able to get them to sit still.

The garment bag held a long, silky, V-necked black dress with three-quarter sleeves, a string of pearls and some simple pearl earrings. I had never worn the dress before. It was one of those things I had bought on a whim, thinking basic black might be useful sometime.

After I changed into my outfit, Michael positioned us on a carpeted platform. Nykey and Maddie circled around me, then settled on the carpet. Michael's wife, Karen, helped to keep them in place.

Michael added a small white column, topped with a vase of well-worn artificial flowers. He noticed my questioning look. He knew I was thinking they looked a little tacky.

"Don't worry, they'll look fine in the photograph."

Michael was right. The picture was perfect. I can't say that Nykey and Maddie looked at me adoringly, but perhaps the painters created those special effects.

* * *

I have my "eighteenth-century" portrait now. It hangs in the upstairs hall of my house where few people see it. It wasn't meant for public view. It's my tribute to the past. A celebration of the time when dogs lost their status as objects and became the beloved companions of humans.

I call it "Woman in Black with Two Labradors."

SECOND CHANCES

Old age means realizing you will never own all the dogs you wanted to.

Joe Gores

Three old ladies.

Different species. Kindred spirits.

Living our second lives.

* * *

Daffy jumped from her transport car and ran across the grass, tail wagging, ready to start her new life with me. Her pink tongue hung sideways in what looked like a smile. She wobbled from side to side with a comical gait, her big paws swinging outward as if they didn't quite know where to put themselves down. What seemed charming and quirky at the time later turned out to be severe arthritis and a damaged spine. But that day, I knew Daffy was perfect.

Daffy spent the first part of her life in an Amish barn in Lancaster County, Pennsylvania. She lived in the straw like the other farm animals, sharing her stall with another dog. She bore litters of puppies for the farmer, who valued them as part of his cash crop. She was about to be sold to another farmer when a Lab Rescue volunteer discovered her.

"If you want this dog, you need to take her today. I'm going to sell her to one of the other farmers who wants to keep on breeding her."

Daffy was eight years old. Her days as a breeding bitch should have been over. Rescue made sure they were.

Old rescue dogs move into their new lives dragging the remnants of their past habits and fears. Daffy is no exception. Even before the human ear can hear thunder, her body starts to tremble. She paces and pants. I give her a sedative and find a quiet place for her to hide from the storm.

But I always wonder. What was it like for Daffy, huddled in that dark barn in Pennsylvania while the storm raged around her? Did the other farm animals comfort her? Did she bury herself deep in the hay in a futile attempt to escape?

I will never know. I only know that Daffy doesn't have to be afraid of thunder anymore.

* * *

Daffy and I were lonely. Raleigh had gone to the Rainbow Bridge. It was just the two of us. The house was much too quiet. I sent an e-mail to the rescue.

Does Lab Rescue have a senior Lab for me?

The hoped-for response came back:

We have a 9-year-old chocolate Lab mix from a shelter in rural Virginia. Her name is Molly. You can see her in Annapolis.

Molly sounded like the one for us. I helped Daffy climb the ramp into the back of the SUV, and we drove to Maryland.

Molly greeted us without fanfare, as if to say, "Well, I'm glad you finally got here. I've been waiting for you." She sniffed Daffy in appropriate doggy fashion. She sniffed my hands and feet. She sniffed my clothes. Molly's nose was clearly an important analytical tool. To our relief, Daffy and I passed the smell test. Molly was ready to adopt us.

I loaded Daffy and Molly into the SUV for the trip home. They curled up together on the dog bed in the back, and before I had driven five miles, they were asleep on top of each other.

I rejoiced. *This merger is going to work. We are a family.*

* * *

Molly's former life is a mystery, but there are clues. An abdomen that looks like an udder. A docked tail. A fresh wound on her chest. And ears that don't look anything like a Lab's.

Molly's ears quickly became a topic of conversation among Lab people. Lab ears aren't supposed to be large and heavy. Molly's were. Very large. Very heavy. The ancestor that gave Molly her ears was definitely not a Lab.

"Could she be part bloodhound?" "Is she mixed with some kind of spaniel?" Everyone had an opinion.

A DNA test solved one part of the mystery. Molly isn't a Lab. She is a pure-bred, German Short-Haired Pointer. The docked tail goes with the breed. Her unusual liver color fooled everyone.

The rest of Molly's former life is an educated guess. Her "udder" tells us that she's had a lot of puppies and was probably a backyard breeder. Did she injure her chest when she escaped her cage? Was she abandoned by an owner who had no use for her anymore?

I will never know. I only know that Molly is living the life she deserves, and there are no more puppies.

* * *

Daffy wobbles on arthritic joints. Molly needs a tummy tuck. I long for the days when I looked good in a bathing suit.

I am no longer the fifties housewife whose proudest accomplishments were a batch of homemade cookies and a finely-stitched seam. Mental illness has altered the direction of my life, just as rescue changed Molly's and Daffy's.

A doctorate from an Ivy League university. A successful professional career. A place in *Who's Who of American Women*. Would they have happened without depression and mania, or in spite of them? Was I lucky enough to find the right medication?

Many victims of bipolar disorder—artists in particular—choose to forgo treatment. They fear that medication will dull the mania that fuels their creative energy to write, compose, or paint. They are willing to accept the inevitable plunges into depression as the price they must pay for creativity.

I have opted for treatment. Pills, yes. But also doses of silky ears, slurpy kisses, and wagging tails. Dogs have been my medicine of choice. They have soothed my pain. They have shared my joy. They have given me purpose. They have truly been the stars of my drama.

* * *

A winter day. We have completed our hasty walks through the falling snow and retreated to the warmth of the fireplace. I slide a favorite old CD into the player, and classical guitar music fills the empty spaces of the room.

Daffy sighs and stretches out on the floor at my feet. Medication and acupuncture keep her free of pain. She quickly falls into a peaceful sleep.

Molly curls her ample body beside me on the sofa, her head in my lap. She snores in contentment. She is in her favorite place.

I reach for my needlepoint project. It will be a pillow:

If you want a friend in Washington, get a dog.

Three old ladies, savoring our second lives.

EPILOGUE

To be with the dog beside me is to stay close to
every dog that went before, a sweet succession…
like April into May, allowing love to overlap.

Unknown

Her name was April Daffodil, but everyone called her Daffy.

She was my sunshine. My inspiration. The smiley, happy girl who hobbled into my heart three years ago and never left. The determined dog who balanced on a big rubber ball and struggled through a tunnel to the cheers of her physical therapist. Who knew that climbing the ramp into the

SUV meant a trip to Dr. Taylor's farm for acupuncture and a visit with the miniature pig?

But she was an old girl too, weakened by her years as a breeder dog in a puppy mill. Along with the good times came disc problems, laryngeal paralysis, and vestibular disease. She coughed and wheezed and panted. She had surgery. The coughing and wheezing and panting continued.

Then came an attack more severe than before. Daffy struggled to breathe. Her tongue and gums turned blue. Her temperature soared. I watched and prayed while the doctors attached IVs, inserted a breathing tube, and gave her CPR. I begged them to keep trying. But they couldn't bring her back. Her thirteen-year-old heart had stopped.

Daffy, my beautiful optimist, was gone.

I buried my face in her soft yellow fur for the last time and sobbed. I stroked her silky ears and velvet muzzle. I looked into her brown eyes, once warm, now clouded and sightless. Daffy would never again look at me and smile.

I forced myself to turn away. There was nothing to do but say good-bye. The pain of Daffy's loss filled my heart and followed me home in the empty car.

Two dogs were waiting for me.

So were the mind gremlins.

Why didn't you do another test?

Why didn't you take her for a consult?

Couldn't you have driven any faster to the hospital?

You should have done more for her.

The gremlins arrive to torture me after every dog's death. They remind me of treatments that I might have done but didn't. They tell me that I have failed my dog. They assure me that I didn't do enough to save her.

They don't leave until the passage of time has smoothed the raw edges of my grief and my veterinarian has assured me, more than once, that I did everything I could. Only then can the rational part of my brain chase them away. Until the next time.

* * *

Daffy is still with me. I vacuum her yellow fur from the carpet, reluctant to empty the canister into the trash. I wash her bed, knowing that it may smell fresh and clean to me, but her scent will remain for the other dogs to remember.

Old habits remain. When it's time to go for a walk, I reach for her leash. I stammer over Molly's name and call her Daffy. At mealtime, I set out three bowls. Tears fill my eyes when I look at the empty space where I once put hers. I wake during the night to listen for her breathing, but the room is silent.

There is comfort in the familiar rituals of grieving. I request a private cremation. I add her picture to the memorial wall. I post her obituary on Facebook, and weep over the messages from friends. I hang her collar on the big hook that holds the collars of the eighteen other dogs that have gone before her.

Daffy is gone, but not the pain.

* * *

Two weeks before Daffy died, there was an e-mail from Lab Rescue:

> *We just rescued a 12-year-old yellow boy whose owners took him to the shelter and said they couldn't care for him any longer. Would you be willing to foster him? His name is Benji.*

I couldn't say no.

Benji met Daffy and Molly with quiet resignation. His eyes were on the ground. His tail sagged between his hind legs. He had none of the joyful enthusiasm of a typical Lab. Benji was depressed. And why not? He had been left in a noisy shelter after twelve years with the only family he had ever known. He didn't know what had happened to him. He didn't know what would happen next. He was confused and afraid.

Benji broke my heart when he stood at my back gate, looking out, as if waiting for someone to come for him. He wouldn't eat. I worked through my repertoire of finicky dog menus to find something that would entice him to take a few bites. Despite several dog beds to choose from, he found a quiet place on the carpeted landing of the stairs between the first and second floors. At night he curled up and slept there, alone.

But after a few days, Benji stopped looking out the gate. He began to eat. He tried out one of the dog beds. He followed me all over the house, his sad amber eyes watching every move as if he were recording it for future reference. He learned to look for dinner at 4:30 p.m. To join Molly at the front door for a long walk in the morning and a short walk in the afternoon. To wait for his medicine wrapped in cheese. And, most important of all, that it was okay to sleep on the family room sofa.

Benji was home. How could I send him away? He belonged with us.

The day after Daffy died there was an afternoon thunder storm. Benji didn't seem to mind it, but Molly paced with anxiety. She usually finds safety in the bathroom or against the sofa at my feet. But that day, she found another refuge.

Benji was in his usual place on the landing. Molly curled up beside him, as if to say:

> I feel safe with you.

* * *

My beloved dogs who have gone before are always close. I feel their presence. Their memories live on in my mind, in my heart, and in the stories I tell. They have brought great joy as well as great sorrow. They have given far more to me than I have ever given to them. It is the lopsided bargain I accepted when I chose to rescue old dogs.

Now my sweet Daffy has joined them.

Molly and Benji are beside me. Are there more to come?

Love never ends. Love overlaps. The sweet succession continues.

Eighty-four paws.

And counting.

THE DOGS WHO HAVE GONE BEFORE

Buddy (July 6, 1999 – October 28, 2002)
Moody (1995 – August 26, 2003)
Siggy (April 28, 1999 – July 9, 2004)

Abbey Belle (December 12, 2002 – April 28, 2003)

Katie (March 19, 2004 – May 14, 2006)
Nykey (June 22, 2004 – June 21, 2010)
Tootsie (August 28, 2003 – August 8, 2007)

Maddie (August 17, 2007 – March 26, 2012)
Nykey (June 22, 2004 – June 21, 2010)
Ginger (September 9, 2006 – March 14, 2008)

The Dogs Who Have Gone Before

Maddie (August 17, 2007 – March 26, 2012)
Homey (June 23, 2009 – October 6, 2009)
Nykey (June 22, 2004 – June 21, 2010)
Buck (January 28, 2009 – July 24, 2010)

Napoleon (April 20, 2009 – May 29, 2009)

Bizzy (April 22, 2011 – February 8, 2012)

Raleigh (June 6, 2009 – October 29, 2016)
Cody (April 4, 2011 – August 3, 2013)
Hope (February 21, 2010 – November 28, 2015)

K.D. (April 19, 2012 – February 22, 2016)
Hope (February 21, 2010 – November 28, 2015)
Raleigh (June 6, 2009 – October 29, 2016)

Raleigh (June 6, 2009 – October 29, 2016)
Hope (February 21, 2010 – November 28, 2015)
K.D. (April 19, 2012 – February 22, 2016)
Quincy (November 26, 2012 – November 8, 2013)

Daffy (February 18, 2015 – August 20, 2018)

THE DOGS WHO ARE WITH ME NOW

Molly (November 13, 2016 – present)
Benji (August 11, 2018 – present)

ACKNOWLEDGEMENTS

At age 84, after a career of writing academic articles and policy statements, I decided to write a book. It wasn't as easy as I thought it might be, but I have had a lot of help. I am so grateful to all of the friends and colleagues who helped me put an idea that burned inside me for a long time, onto the printed page.

This book would not have been possible at all without the expertise of my very special friends and Lab lovers, Juana Green-Nicoletta and Matthew Nicoletta. Juana has not only been my editor, but also my mentor and critic. Matt devoted his marketing and computer skills to turn a concept into a reality.

I owe much to Carolyn Page, who teaches Creative Writing in the Fairfax, Virginia, Adult Education Program. I took her course three times. She scolded and prodded and made me think. After the third try I felt as if I just might be able to write. I hope she will be pleased with her student's progress.

I am most appreciative of the support I have received from two writing groups, The Writers of Chantilly and the Oakton Writers Group. They have listened to my writing and given me kind constructive feedback. Their comments have been invaluable.

Dr. Richard Roth does not make an appearance in my book, but his presence is always felt. He has been my psychiatrist for more than 25 years. His calm demeanor and intellect—and his willingness to talk about Labs—have kept me sane.

Although she is no longer with us, I must remember Norma Newmark, my mentor and friend. She opened the door into a world I had not known before, and introduced me to the richness of life as a liberated woman—a life that has included my beloved old Labs.

Ever since Moody started his treatment for heartworm many years ago, the doctors and staff at Centerville Animal Hospital have provided loving care for my Labs. They have nursed them back to health, and they have been there when it was time to say goodbye.

Finally, this book would not exist without the wonderful Labs who have come to me through Lab Rescue LRCP, an organization for which I volunteered for more than twenty years. My gratitude goes to all the volunteers of Lab Rescue who love the seniors as much as I do, and who have helped me find them.

PHOTO CREDITS

Unless otherwise noted here, all photographs were provided courtesy of the author.

Page 1: Pet Portraits by Michael

Page 39: Pet Portraits by Michael

Page 87: Pet Portraits by Michael

Page 125: Juana Green-Nicoletta

Page 137: Pet Portraits by Michael

Page 139: Pet Portraits by Michael

Page 145: Pet Portraits by Michael

Page 157: Juana Green-Nicoletta

Page 159 (top): Pet Portraits by Michael

Page 160 (top): Pet Portraits by Michael

Page 161: Pet Portraits by Michael

Page 171: Fuzzypants Pet Photography

Page 175: Pet Portraits by Michael

Page 177: Juana Green-Nicoletta

Back Cover: Juana Green-Nicoletta

ABOUT THE AUTHOR

Barbara Travis Osgood is a native New Yorker who earned her PhD in Human Ecology at Cornell University. She retired as a Senior Executive with the Natural Resources Conservation Service, U.S. Department of Agriculture, in 2002. For more than twenty years, her passion has been fostering and rescuing old Labrador Retrievers. Dr. Osgood lives in Fairfax, Virginia, with her current old Labs, Molly and Benji.

Made in the USA
Columbia, SC
21 September 2022

67642579R00114